Conquer Your Fear of Failure

Escape Your Comfort Zone, Overcome Anxiety, Take Action Despite Being Scared, and Reinvent A Fearless You.

SOM BATHLA

www.sombathla.com

Your Free Gift

As a token of my thanks for taking out time to read my book, I would like to offer you a free gift:

Click Below and Download your **Free Report**

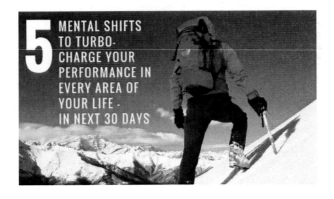

Learn 5 Mental Shifts To Turbo-Charge Your Performance In Every Area Of Your Life - in Next 30 Days!

You can also grab your FREE GIFT Report through this below URL:

http://sombathla.com/mentalshifts

Content

Part I: Introduction

"One who fears failure limits his activities. Failure is only the opportunity to more intelligently begin again." Henry Ford

"What If I FALL?"–Avoid or Embrace

I recalled a scene from my childhood when watching a movie. The movie clip was something like this.

A man was walking on a wall. The height of the wall seemed around five feet, and it was about two feet wide. The man appeared to be comfortable walking on the wall. While walking, he was talking to one of his students just standing below—seemingly; he was explaining something to the student. A few moments later, the teacher asked the student, "Can you come up and walk on this wall with me?"

The student looked at the wall and said, "Not a big deal, sir. I can come and walk."

Then the teacher held the student's hand and picked him up. The moment the student stood up on the wall, he was shocked and started trembling.

I was surprised. Why? What would have happened to this young man?

Then, as it happens in the movies, they showed the bigger picture. The wall was, in fact, a huge wall of a big old fort. And this little five feet wall on one side had a deep valley on its other side. It was so deep that there was no possibility for survival if someone ever falls into it. Obviously, the immediate thought the student had was,"***What if I fall?***"

Not just that student, the younger me also got spooked after seeing the glimpse of the depth of the valley even on the screen. Honestly, even today, if I look down from my balcony— just from the tenth floor, I become overwhelmed by the fear of heights.

Above was a frightening movie scene I recollected from the past. Then I instantly thought of the feelings, which arise from another common real-life situation and which is also about falling but gives an entirely different message.

Okay, let's take one daily life example

You and I have seen toddlers when they crawl on the ground. Then, on one fine day, they start trying to stand up on their small feet. They are trying to put the whole load of their entire body on their two feet—two small feet. It is a big move, at least for them, right? The entire body, which was so far being supported by four body parts, will now be solely handled by two small feet. It is a 200% load for legs first of all, and the double whammy is that it is for the first time—no experience of past at all.

Now see what happens next. The child tries to stand up, and she falls. But, it doesn't matter for her—she giggles funnily and again tries. Oh God, she again falls. She tries more, she falls. It is not 1 or 2 or 4 times. It is 30, 40, or maybe 50 times, she falls. Sometimes, she might get tiny bruises here and there and cries loudly, and sometimes she just laughs on her falls. But this falling continues.

What a level of patience she has got. Falling so many times, but handling it with a laugh, giggle, cry and it continues until one fine day, when she gets up on her legs—yes, by herself on her own two legs.

And this journey again starts from standing on her own feet until walking on her feet and then running on her feet. With numerous fallings going on and on!

Now, this was another example of—"**What if I fall?**"

Think about the difference in both the scenarios stated above. It is quite obvious to assess the impact of both the falls. So what is the message here?

The falling in the first case was fatal for sure, and one will surely lose a very precious gift called Life. The falling in the second case was nowhere near fatal at all; rather this falling was necessary for the kid to start learning to stand on her own feet and then walk.

While the first falling was worth avoiding, the second falling was worth seeking. Therefore, every fall cannot be considered as a failure. Rather some falls are necessary for your journey to success. You can comfortably bet that there is no human being on this planet who has started walking on his feet directly without a single fall. Rather this failure by way of falling is instrumental to gradually build the child's strength and rising to her feet. The same analogy applies to few failures on our way to our goals, but the irony is that we are prepared to give up only after one or two failures. Imagine the poor kid giving up her hope of walking after the first two falls; you would be watching an entirely different breed of human beings—crawling on their fours like animals.

"Our greatest glory is not in never falling, but in rising every time we fall." Confucius

Let me be candid here. This book is not about fear of those life-threatening failures and how to address those. Your brain is already well-equipped (with pre-installed mechanism) with an almond-shaped mass of gray material in your brain called the amygdala, to keep you safe from all such life-threatening experience (more on the amygdala later). In fact, this is the amygdala which had protected the human species to survive in those primitive ages when a man was always surrounded by wild animals in the jungle and always subject to dangers.

This book is written primarily to help you look at the fear of failure differently. The key tenet of this book is to enable you to understand your fear of failure and, more particularly, develop a different kind of relationship with failure. You will understand that some fallings or failures are utmost necessary and must be experienced before you can achieve any measurable success.

A Real-Life Failure Tragedy
There was some suicide incident I heard in the news a few years ago. A student in a high school in northern part of India committed suicide after seeing his examination results. It

was revealed that this student was studying hard to get good results so that he could become eligible for better colleges in his pursuit for higher education. He was expecting 98% in the examination, which as per his research was necessary for getting admissions in any good institution. But when the result came out, he failed to meet his own expectation. He was able to score only 96% marks. But in his mind, he had failed. He couldn't digest this failure and therefore committed suicide.

Why did this boy take such a horrible step to end his life?

Because this was the definition of failure, this boy had thought in his mind. He had dreams to be admitted to the best institutions in the country, and a score of 98% or above was his only and limited definition of success. But when his dream of getting admission to his preferred institution appeared to be out of his reach, he might have thought that he was not good enough, and that's why he had failed. His limited and myopic vision of life made him so convinced that there was no meaning left in his life.

What is your reaction to this? Most of us would empathize with the poor student, who ended his life, even before it started. Any reasonable man would say: this cannot be the reason for ending one's life. In my view, there can't be any good reason to end one's life, no matter what happens.

But this young man forgot that if one door gets closed in life then many others get opened. This is the way life works. There are tons of examples in history when people have shifted their entire careers and achieved massive success arising out of their failure (stay with me, you will see many such examples in the book later). In fact, the scope of admission to the best institutions in the country was not yet ruled outfor him entirely. In such case, some students skip one year of their further education, re-appear in the same class with full fledged preparations, and then are able to score higher marks in the next year. So, it was just an additional effort of one year of life, but this young man chose to end his precious life say seventy years prematurely. It was really a bad mathematical calculation.

Life is Like a Game of Cricket

Life is similar to the game of cricket. In this game, you are the batsman and life is a bowler. Life will keep throwing balls at you, and you have to play it. But there is one advantage in this life game—because some rules are more advantageous to you. Unlike the game of cricket, you don't have three stumps (called wickets) behind you, which if touched by the ball, you get out of the game. Therefore, if you try your best to hit the ball right in the middle of your bat and even if somehow miss hitting the ball, then don't worry—you won't get out.

Therefore, the advantage of this game of life is that you can keep practicing and try your best to hit the balls coming to you every time. Sometimes you can hit the ball for six or four runs, but sometimes the ball goes empty. But here is the good part—you don't get out of the game. You get OUT of the game or lose the game only if you quit and leave the ground.

Therefore, in order to win this game of life, you just have to stick to the ground and keep hitting the balls that life throws toward you. You have to keep hitting, and with practice, you will be hitting most of the balls of life and succeed. The missed balls will teach you that your positioning or your timing was not correct, and you can learn from your mistakes.

"When we give ourselves permission to fail, we, at the same time, give ourselves permission to excel." - Eloise Ristad

Who Needs This Book More?

At the outset, let me clarify that "What If I Fail?" could have two different interpretations, which I want to distinguish here clearly, and two different types of people will approach them differently.

The first category of people comprises of those who, whenever they come across anything new, get into a fearful state of mind. The new thing could be as small as talking to a stranger, saying hi to someone of the opposite sex, or as big as proposing to the person you love to marry you, appearing for a competitive exam, showing up for a job interview, or starting a new business. Or it could be anything new, which you face at any point in your life. The instant reaction of this category of people is fear. They get fearful and anxious as to what would happen if they fail. The people who fall into this category have a very narrow definition of failure. To them, "fear" means something very bad and unacceptable, which they must avoid experiencing at all cost. For them, failure appears like a stigma on their personality. They see it as a white label pasted on their forehead stating, "I am a failure," which will make them a laughing stock in the eyes of surrounding people. So these people have the first and instant reaction to avoid anything new or uncomfortable, and they rather choose to stay in their cocoon of self-made comfort.

The target audience of this book is this first category of people. Why? I will describe it once I have explained the second category of people.

This second category of people comprises of courageous people. They are afraid of failure to some extent, but they use their courage muscle to stand in front of fear. Now when these people are faced with any such new thing, they also think in their mind, "What If I Fail?" But the interpretation of "What If I Fail?" is completely different. It is a very factual and straightforward question. They are simply asking what is "the next step?" if they fail at this endeavor in front of them.

How is it different from the first category? Let me explain here.

You can see, the first category of people *only* think about what would happen if they fail and then see all kind of negative scenarios in front of them. The result is that they stop at this thinking stage and don't take any action at all. But this second category of people is willing to take action, but mindful that things may not go as they would want, so *"what if I fail?"* is their question about the backup plan for them. To put it succinctly:

Category 1 *--> Think 'What if I fail?' -->* <u>*Get plagued & don't start*</u>

Category 2 *--> Think 'What if I fail?' -->* <u>*Start the work with a backup plan (if they fail)*</u>

Let me elaborate this by telling about an example in my own life. In my last few years of my corporate career, I was always thinking of shifting the gears and starting my own business. It didn't occur to me until much later what the right path for me was. But once I got some initial clarity that probably generating valuable content to inspire the world was the immediate best thing that I could do to at least start.

Let me be honest. I was in the first category of people then. Strangely, even after taking massive action in that direction, I found myself in the first category. How? Let me peel the layers of inner psychology at that time. By the latter half of 2014, I had written my first book, *The 30-Hour Day*.

Here is what I did. I didn't publish the books for two weeks, despite it being fully ready. Why?

I was fearful and thinking, what if people don't like it? What if it affects my career in the corporate world? What if it affects my job?

What if people laugh at me about what I was doing it? What if it doesn't generate the revenue I was expecting to sustain a full-time career? What if I get confused about my real identity, i.e., lawyer versus author? I think there were some more what ifs, but I think this much is enough to convey my inner fearful emotional journey to you.

Somehow, after a lot of debates with my inner critic, I published my first book on Amazon after two weeks. Though you might laugh at me, let me expose myself more. I was so scared for next six weeks about people coming to know about it. Why? Again due to the above: what ifs. I know for some of you, it might sound foolish—you would think, what is so scary about this—if you are exposing yourself and imparting some inspirational message to the world (people these days even publish non-sensible YouTube videos without a flinch).

Somehow, I gathered courage at the end of 2014, and wrote an email to five people with a link to my book to check what they thought about it (four of which were my relatives). Within the next hour, I got a call from all of them expressing how proud of me they were about what I had accomplished. I realized that I have formally put myself as an author on the world's biggest online bookstore. Then I did some marketing activities to promote my book at the store, and the book touched #1 at Amazon in the Time Management category.

My fears didn't leave me even here. At such occasion, when most people would have blasted their social media networks about this mega achievement, I was like hiding in a cave. I just shared the news with a limited number of people, and that's it.

Why this again? Now a new fear—that it might affect my job, as they might have thought that I had been engaged in some other revenue-generating activity without their permission. I knew somehow that it was an irrational fear (as I had done everything related to writing my book over my weekends, evenings, and late nights-, never at the company's cost or time, nor in any competitive field—it was just like trading in stocks in my free time or investing somewhere in my free time).

You can see that I was in the first category of people, i.e., scared of failing in author career and then assuming that it would be the end of the world.

Now, as my life unfolded, new circumstances arrived and everything outside seemed to not go according to my values of freedom and adventure. Suddenly, reaching the top rungs of the corporate ladder was appearing to be not a worthy pursuit. I couldn't see my superiors at the organization I was working, as my ideals to follow. Their way of working and their lifestyle didn't inspire me much to follow that route. Also, the corporate environment, unfruitful office gossiping, and politics didn't seem to be worth putting in the effort, despite knowing the fact that these are one of the necessary ingredients if you wish to accelerate your journey to higher echelons of the organization.

Thankfully, now I was in the second category of people. Now I was thinking of seriously starting my own writing career or something else in the online world to do justice with my ultimate life values of freedom and adventure. I don't know if it was good or bad, but my spouse had entirely opposite life values (she wanted security and certainty) by way of a regular paycheck every month. So, the journey started from (a) "knowing" my and my wife's values first, (b) then working for a few years to test my values on my own and endless debates with my spouse to arrive at some conclusion on our conflicting life values. All this led to reinforcing my belief and my conviction about pursuing my life values. So I think this disagreement between our values was good for me because I could make a clear distinction between my real values, due to my living by the others values (which I was not convinced).

I realized that "things don't happen *to* me, things happen *for* me,"—as is quoted by some great soul.

Why I explained so much about my values is because of this one thing: if you get clarity, you will have half the battle won already, because then these values will pull you toward the life you want with double the amount of force. Suddenly, you will feel that you put just one foot forward and your values pull you two steps ahead.

Okay, coming to the second category of people, which I had now traveled. Now my question was again, "What if I fail?"

I hope you know what tone it was now. I didn't doubt myself. I asked a *'factual'* question to myself, *"What will I do if I fail?* Then I picked my factual answer, i.e., arranged the necessary funds to focus on my writing career until I got enough readers to support my family and to occasionally have a nice dinner with family or few beers with friends. Frankly, I didn't think much about going back again because looking backward didn't seem an inspiring move to me (I know based on my discussions with corporate colleagues in the past that most of them didn't have any inspiration and suffered from the "Monday blues"). Although I did not have any credentials or success in my forthcoming career as an author (except having written just one book), I had great faith that things will improve if I keep moving. I had only to figure out how to survive for some time until I get something rolling.

I hope I was able to make you understand the deep message out of my story. Just to summarize, the message was two-fold.

Number 1: I was trying to explain the difference between two sets of people, who look at "What if I fail?" in two different ways.

Number 2: The mission of this book will be primarily to address the mental state of the first category of people. It touches upon the psychological issues and the internal struggles going on in the heads of people while thinking of their worth pursuing life goals. Because, as is rightly stated:

"Your inner game dictates your outer game" ~ Fabienne Fredrickson

In fact, the people in the second category have tamed their fear of failure to a large extent, as they have used their courage to face fears and overcome them. They only need a plan to move ahead, if things don't move according to their desired plan.

What Is The Purpose Of This Book?

I am writing this book with the objectives, as listed below:

a. I care about my readers and therefore want to change your perspective about what you think about failure and the fear of failure. I want you to look at the failure as an ally and a stepping stone for success. This book will help you to embrace your fears; you will move towards your fear of failure rather than get repelled from them once you understand the real purpose of failure in your journey. Yes, I want you to realize that failure is something that serves multiple purposes in your life, one of which is to achieve success and then sustain the earned success. I don't want your success to be like winning a lottery. I want your success to be a success, which remains with you for life, even if you lose your entire empire, you should be able to create the same again with your upgraded mindset and beliefs about failure.

b. Secondly, I don't merely want to motivate you; rather I want you to get access to the practical ways and means to start implementing the same as you keep on reading this book. I believe that you don't need more and more motivation at an intellectual level, but you need to arouse your experiential awareness about what you have learned so far. What I want for you out of this book is that you should think of moving immediately and start taking action toward your goals. What I want of you is no more living on false fears and excuses. I don't want you to justify yourself to live a mediocre life. I want you to be one of those distinguished few, who have understood their gift that God has given to them. I want you to be one among those, who have opened their wrappers and have seen inside the gleaming gift of their being. As someone rightly stated:

"Everyone is gifted, but most people never open their package." ~ *Anonymous*

Why Should You Listen To Me?

If you are reading my book for the first time, I briefly want to introduce myself. I am passionate about exploring the limitlessness of human potential. My exploration instincts and my curiosity had made me read hundreds of books on personal development, human psychology, peak performance, and how to master time and energy to get the best out of being human. I read and started implementing those principles in my life in general and in the corporate world, where I worked for around 17 years. Once I tested a principle in one area and got some success, I implemented the same in another areas and found some results.

So far, I have written more than half a dozen books on various aspects of life, ranging from time management, productivity, mastering focus, to deeper and also darker aspects of human psychology like conquering self-doubt. My recent books, *The Mindset Makeover*, *Living Beyond Self Doubt* and a few others have already touched Amazon #1 Bestseller rank. You can find more details about me and my books at www.sombathla.com.

My work experiences in the corporate world, my life experiences and implementation of wisdom gems learned from others into my personal life make me eligible to write and publish the books on personal growth including the current book in your hand. My premise of writing is to share real-life stories, tell about my personal experiences, and then to convey my message to people who are seeking some actionable steps to move ahead in life.

So, are you ready?

Let's continue the journey towards conquering the fear of failure.

****

Part II: "What If I Fail?" Syndrome- Deconstructed

"What would life be if we had no courage to attempt anything?" ~ Vincent van Gogh

Where Does This Fear Come From?

It is not suddenly that on one fine day you wake up and start doubting yourself and your abilities to succeed in your goals or dreams. Rather, this is a gradual deterioration of your thinking process, in which you have been engaged for many years on a day to day basis. Your thinking and mindset get plagued with doubts, fears, and insecurities because of the surrounding environment in which you live.

So you would feel that it is not your fault and you are completely innocent. But hang on! You might have started your journey as innocent, but later on, it is only you who is the perpetrator for getting into this fearful state. Let me explain it a bit.

You were innocently trapped into a mediocre way of thinking through your environment that you should be scared of failing. The definition of failure was explained to you as if you would fall from a huge fort wall – as you read in the previous section. Though, your parents were seemingly very happy to see you falling again and again when you were learning to stand up and walk. They were quite happy when you were learning to ride a bicycle and were falling quite often.

You still recall your mother or father applying balm on your bruises—but at the same time saying that you shouldn't bother about these wounds and bruises. Rather you were told that it is fine to fall often when you are trying to learn. Most parents seem to tell their kids that they only succeed after falling. This is such a great piece of education, isn't it?

But here's the catch. Your parents were only teaching to you what they had learned from their parents, society, and environment. Unfortunately, this good education stops after learning a few necessary skills—necessary in our understanding in order to live our day to day lives. But when it comes to applying this psychology to your bigger life questions, most parents have not even themselves gathered much education about how to drive the life further to a much higher level. I am not putting the entire blame on our parents, but just trying to lay out the facts. Most parents just don't know, because they were not taught by their environment on how to face and rather welcome rejections in life.

They may not have learned well—that if you are rejected in life, that's also fine—like falling from a bicycle. The scenario changes entirely now—they don't tell you to go and do the things which you love to do—the majority of parents don't want their kids to become a musician, sports player, artist, painter, poet, etc. They don't tell you to go and propose the person you like and talk to him. They don't tell you to try different businesses at an early age, or tell you that only failing quite often would lead you to success in your business.

Why it is so that the same parents, who were feeling happy to see you standing up on your feet, walking, and riding a bicycle—and also soothing your wounds—suddenly become so hypersensitive about you and don't want you to fail anymore?

Why do they tell you to do what the crowd does? Why do they preach to you to go to school, get good grades, secure an education loan, get a good job, get a house and mortgage, keep repaying the loans and make some savings, retire—and that's it?

A few reasons:

    a. They learned the same ideals from their parents and are just passing the baton to the next generation.

    b. They didn't experience newer things beyond basic life skills, like riding a bicycle, so they are also scared and skeptical about anything new or bigger.

    c. Since they are fearful about the future and had led a safe (but slow) life, they want the same for you as well—you know, they are your well-wishers.

I read an Indian mythological instance in Mahabharata, an Indian scripture. It went something like this.

Arjuna and Krishna were passing through a village. On the way, Arjuna saw a cow, which was licking its young calf's body out of love. But the irony was, it was licking the calf with so much intensity that the calf was hurting at places and it was bleeding too. Arjuna asked Krishna, "Lord, why do you think this cow is licking its child so much that it is getting hurt?"

Krishna told Arjuna that it was about the change of Yuga (meaning 'ages' or 'eras') and this indicates that parents will be loving and caring their children so much that this would even be hurting the children. But the irony is that the parent has a strong belief that he was taking care of the child.

But I would like to make it clear here; you should not blame your parents for their point of view. There is an expiry date on blaming your parents for steering you in the wrong direction; the moment you are old enough to take the wheel, responsibility lies with you.

Yes, we agree that you were influenced by the mindset and belief system of your society, your parents, and your environment. But it has to stop somewhere. You have an independent mind, your own consciousness, and you have to see the world with your own unique perspective.

How long will you keep making excuses? Why can't you lead your life like learning to ride the bicycle?

The bicycle is a great analogy to learn how to live your life, for many reasons:

a. You have to continuously balance your bicycle on the road.
b. You need to understand course-correction while on the move: you need to keep the handlebar left, right, or straight in order to balance yourself and also to ensure that the bicycle keeps moving.

c. You don't know about the road and the pitfalls coming your way, so you learn to face uncertainty.

d. Over a period of regular riding, you get the experience as to what kind of pitfalls come and how to avoid falling into that.

But instead of riding a bicycle, you have chosen to live your life on crutches—crutches of the old belief system you borrowed from your parents, society, and surrounding environment. Crutches of certain but slower life paths. Crutches of the comfort of the known, but devoid of any personal life experiences.

Crutches keep you safe and comfortable. You don't get hurt with the support of crutches, but you also don't walk faster. You don't get to see the exciting places with crutches. Of course, you don't fall, but you compromise your rise as well with the crutches.

Your old and borrowed belief systems are your crutches, which you should throw on the side and roll up your sleeves to pick up your courage bicycles and start living a life of amazement.

"Life is like riding a bicycle. To keep your balance, you must keep moving."
~ Albert Einstein

What Is the Role of the Amygdala— the Fear Center of the Brain?

If you are not already aware, the fear center of our brain is the amygdala. It is an almond-shaped mass of gray material in your brain, and the prime function of this part of the brain is to send you the signals of fight or flight or freeze, in the case of a situation of danger. In fact, this element of fear is one of the basic and necessary ingredients for our survival.

The role of this part of the brain was much more relevant in the primitive age when a human being was living in jungles. There was always a fear of any tiger or lion jumping at you in search for food. So your life was always at stake—as it could have easily become prey to any wild animal, had you not been alert enough. The role of the amygdala is to trigger the neurons in your brain to send the signals to your heart to beat faster and your body to make a quick decision about fight or flight or freeze.

But the role of the amygdala in modern life is very limited. The majority of the world's population is quite safe these days, except a few countries, where there is still terrorism and wars going on. You don't live in jungles anymore and are not prone to any physical attacks. Rather, you stay in relatively safe apartments or houses; your workplaces are safe. You are not always in an imminent danger.

But, despite the above, we cannot totally overrule the significance of fear. Fear is still one of the most important elements to keep us protected from life-threatening dangers. We cannot blindly say that there is no fear, and that we should be fearless in all situations.

There was a study[i] conducted on a patient who had damaged her amygdala in some injury. To provoke fear in the patient, the researchers exposed her to live snakes and spiders, took her on a tour of a haunted house, and showed her emotionally evocative films, but the patient didn't exhibit fear on any of the occasions.

You see, this was a study conducted in a research environment. Had this been all real, the situation could have been quite dangerous to this woman, who was not able to receive any life-threatening or hurting signals. For want of any danger signs, her brain couldn't prompt any necessary life-saving actions of flight or fight or freeze.

There was one other study conducted, where the amygdala of a few people was

---

[i] http://www.cell.com/current-biology/fulltext/S0960-9822(10)01508-3

anaesthetized for some time. In that state, some dangerous-looking people were sent to this group of people. There were no signs of any fear on their faces or body language of this group, and they even revealed highly sensitive information, like credit card details, etc. to the strangers. There was no sensation of fear in the mind of this group of people, to even lose their money—that is the impact of a non-functioning amygdala.

Therefore, the amygdala certainly needs to perform its role to protect us from falling from heights, giving us signals to stay away from deep waters or wild animals or insects, and even safeguarding us from loss of our assets.

Yes, you and I can safely conclude that most of the above-stated dangers were more frequent in the past ages as compared to the current modern day technology-driven environment. If you are reading this book on your smartphone or electronic device, it means you have access to electricity, internet, and online banking, so it means your day to day life is pretty much safe without any life threats to you. Also, in some cases, if you are in some unfamiliar territories or out of your comfort areas, some kinds of fears are necessary to safeguard yourself.

But the problem with the modern-day man is that he has started looking at most of the situations of his life with the same intensity as if he would be falling from heights, drowning in deep waters, or being robbed. Below are some kinds of modern-day fears:

a. What if I fail to convince my boss about raising my salary, and she then feels different about me?
b. What if I am not able to convince my prospective client about my credentials?
c. What if I couldn't pass this examination?
d. What if I am not able to clear the job interview for my dream job?
e. What if I propose to this handsome-looking man or a beautiful girl and he or she rejects me?

These fears have the effect of a sweating forehead, wet palms, dry throat, etc. as if a failure in such activities would be a danger to life.

You see, none of these fears or "what ifs" will put you in imminent danger of your life. Of course, the negative outcome disturbs your mental state of affairs, but there is nothing from outside which could harm you. There may be some temporary setbacks in life, but again all this can be handled with some mind-training techniques (which will be covered later in this book). In fact, this requires some discipline in the utilization of our mental faculties by way of regular practices.

You should know that like the amygdala, there is another portion of our brain called the pre-frontal cortex, which helps us to make all our key decisions. It does all the thinking and all the heavy-duty work of the analysis of the situation and helps you make the decision. Unfortunately, this portion of the brain is lazy by nature and needs some effort and discipline to put this portion to work.

Actually what happens is—whenever you don't discipline yourself and activate your pre-frontal cortex to take charge of the situation, the amygdala takes it over and starts releasing fear neurons in your brain. It starts showing you all the bad that might happen to you if you fail at something. Unless controlled, it starts to magnify the negative outcomes as if it is like falling from a height. Therefore, over a period by way of habitual thinking, you tend to keep strengthening the neurons firing up to strengthen your emotions of fear. Only until you take effective actions will you overcome this situation.

What are Your Reasons for Fear of Failure?

Now, let's try to look inside your head to assess what prompts you to think in the first place that you will fail even before attempting.

You know your entire life is made up of the memories and experiences gained. Therefore, whenever you have to make a decision, your mind immediately retrieves the information from the past to take a cue from the past decision—you know our mind is a lazy creature and doesn't want to work much. Therefore, it is important to realize that if your past decisions are not that good, they will not guide you further for a better life.

You would say that the above is quite a general kind of statement. Yes, I agree, and therefore, in this section, we will specifically list out some of the most common reasons that prompts the fear of failure. You might relate to some reasons closely—but other reasons might seem absurd to you. Still, I will list out and elaborate based on the wisdom shared by great thinkers and combine them with my thought process and experiences.

So let's look at each of the reasons one by one.

1. You are trying something entirely new.

There could appear some genuine cases when you feel the fear of failure more. If you are trying something new altogether, the fear of failure is bound to come. If you are going to take some competitive examination for the first time; if you are interviewing for your first job; if you have a very important client meeting, which can significantly improve your business; if you are thinking of quitting your job and starting a new business venture; or if you are thinking of proposing to the person you love to spend the rest of their life with you—such things occur in life for most people. And undoubtedly these situations are very important for growth in one's life.

But new wouldn't mean like launching a spaceship to the planet Jupiter. Such kinds of gigantic idea are also "new" things to be experimented by some adventurous people like Elon Musk, an American business magnate. But if you are reading this book, I can do some wild guessing that you don't have such a mega "dent-in-the-universe" kind of new thing planned for your life. There is a reason behind my wild guess—because if one is thinking of such an earth-shattering new idea, he or she might have already crossed stages of many failures and in all probability wouldn't need to read about overcoming the fear of failure.

Let's admit this. No one likes failure in life. It feels bad. It sucks, of course. You wouldn't want ever to celebrate your failures. You won't be enjoying and throwing a party upon failing, so we all want to avoid failing by all means. But the thing is that we don't have control over everything around us and sometimes, even if you have put your best foot forward, still you don't succeed.

Please be mindful that whenever we come across some new activity, which we have not handled in the past, this kind of fear or stress is almost bound to arise in your mind. On the contrary, this fear of failing is somewhat essential, as this generates a stress in your body and mind, which often makes you move and take requisite steps to move on that activity. Tim Ferriss in his bestseller book the *The 4-Hour Workweek* has stated this kind of stress as "EuStress," meaning beneficial or good stress. Because if you don't feel any stress, then either you are ignorant of the activities involved and taking it very lightly or else you have already handled that activity multiple times—which therefore isn't a new activity for you.

In a nutshell, if you are fearful of an activity that is new and you are doing it for the first time, don't be frightened. It's natural to fear, but you have to stay in the game. Nothing is to be done from outside; rather you just have to control your reaction to the situation. As Charles R. Swindoll has rightly stated:

"Life is 10% what happens to you and 90% how you react to it."

2. You doubt your credentials.

Sometimes you get scared that you don't have the right kind of credentials and you have doubts in your head about your competence or capability and thus feel the fear of failure.

Let me tell you, even when you have enough credentials in your name, you still haven't handled everything in this world. The other day, I was just reading the entertainment section of the newspaper. I read that one of the most established actors was stating that even after so many successful movies, he still gets anxious whenever his new movie is about to release. I was surprised to read that. Why would someone feel the fear or anxiety? Then I realized that every movie is a new movie for the actor and though past successes help to attract the audience, it is about their performance in the current movie, which makes them feel nervous about the release.

Moreover, you would always be short of credentials in something or some manner in your life. But if you haven't done anything specific in the past, that doesn't mean that you can't do it now, because everything happens for the first time in life for everyone.

I remember my experience during my consulting job in the past. Our firm had not done work on this specific type of regulatory affair in its past, and now a client has approached us to get that work done. We didn't say that we have not done that type of work yet, but we accepted the work from the client.

Though my firm had credentials for most of the work in the corporate field, it didn't have the relevant credentials or the requisite client list to show to the client about expertise in that specific area. But somehow, the client approached us about this assignment for seeking that regulatory approval, based on the firm's overall credentials.

Now, it is interesting how we handled the situation. The moment we had a sign that the client would give the work to us, we geared up fast. Some team members had immediately visited the regulatory office and met the specific official about the process. We reviewed every piece of information on the official website of the government department and other reliable sources to get the information; we also explored our connections who had handled that kind of work in the past. Based on all that research, we presented a detailed memo to the client about the complete process for seeking the regulatory approvals.

And good news! The client was impressed after reading our work and happily engaged our firm to get that work done. So not having credentials is not a challenge in my view— if you are willing to put in the necessary work required in some area. And that is the way you keep on adding credentials to your portfolio.

3. You have not succeeded significantly in the past.

Since you think that you have not tasted a major success in some area of your life so far, you think that the future is going to be same.

It may be the case that you are not able to treat many events of your past as successes. Maybe you have forgotten them or those events don't fit into your definition of success. Let me assure you; you have already got enough success in the past. Let's count a few for you.

You have for sure studied for and passed some exams, which is why you can read this book.

You are capable of reading; you are capable of doing the online transaction to buy this book, which means you have a bank account and a credit card in your name. But you don't count them as your successes. You have to view it from a different angle, and you will find people who are not capable of this even. So in the eyes of this latter category of people, you are a success. So success is a subjective term.

I don't know you or your life or work experience, and still, I was able to find some success in your life. Perhaps you should do some introspection; you would certainly be able to find some more success. I believe you will be able to count some success. But if you are still not sure, do not worry. You can immediately start to redefine your past starting tomorrow.

How?

You should start making your today a bit more successful, and then when you look back, you will find yourself a bit more successful with each passing day.

"Just because the past didn't turn out the way you wanted it to, doesn't mean the future can't be better than you ever imagined." ~ Anonymous

There could be reasons that you have not succeeded in the past, which you need to analyze. Maybe you have repeated a mistake a number of times in your life, and that's why you are not getting different results. If that is the case, then you must keep in mind this quote from the legendary Albert Einstein:

"Doing the same things over and over again and expecting different results is the definition of insanity."

Therefore, in my view, the fear of failure about not succeeding in the past cannot withstand longer if you are committed to taking different and better actions today.

4. You don't consider yourself worthy of success.

That's a big problem. You doubt yourself in your own head. Look at this statement below as an instant answer:

"If you don't believe yourself, why should anyone else?" ~*Teresa Mummert*

In fact, this question is the problem with the majority of the population, and it warrants a full book on this subject. Realizing that, I had written the book, *Living Beyond Self Doubt,* which is well-received by readers. You may want to have a look at that if you are truly serious about over-coming self-doubt. You will learn how so many people, who were at the gravest level of depression in their lives and even thinking of committing suicide—due to this plaguing disease of self-doubt—have finally come out and not only survived but have thrived in life with flying colors.

So the fear of not being good enough requires inner clarity, and it is more of a psychological issue rather than anything else.

You won't be the first on this planet to tell yourself that you are worthy of something big, even if you don't believe this.

"I am greatest; I said that even before I knew I was." ~ Muhammad Ali

Therefore if you are scared of failure based on your self-assessment of not being worthy, nothing is going to move until you believe in yourself. Don't worry, if you suffer from lack of self-worth and therefore fearful of taking action, I am mindful of your feelings and emotions. With deep care and respect for you, I have written the last section of the book with various proven strategies to help you move forward.

For now, let's continue to list some other reasons why people are afraid of failure.

5. Nobody tells that you have succeeded.

You fear failure because no one in your world has ever told you that you had succeeded in life in some manner for quite a long time.

You remember that in school, you were given certificates that you have passed this class and now you have to move to the next one, so you consider this success. But once you cross the stage of school or college, no one is going to come to you on a regular basis to tell you if you succeeded or not. In a job, at the max, you get your annual performance appraisal once in a year, but that once-a-year assessment (which also may be biased depending upon your rapport with your superiors) does not help you move the needle significantly.

You must realize that everybody is running their race and doesn't have time to tell you about your success, except those very few who are close to you.

The other reason could be that you have been taking such a safe approach that nobody even noticed anything significant about your progress. Merely waking up, going to work, eating, and sleeping doesn't catch the attention of people. So maybe be you have not done anything truly significant so far in your life, which would have warranted some big applause for you so far.

But this is a chicken and egg situation, my friend. What do you think should happen first? Should people tell you something first or should you first do something worth noticing?

If you think people should tell you something, then you would start doing something, that's not going to happen. Firstly, you have to do something that should trigger the people to tell you about that. The answer is quite straightforward here. It is all about you taking action first. You have to make some noise by your action; only then will people make some noise by their words.

6. And the list can go on and on.

Okay, you may have seventeen more reasons that you think you will fail, but I am convinced that the root cause in most of the cases will boil down to your thinking and approach to handling the situation. You have to take responsibility for your life.

As Oprah Winfrey has aptly stated:

"You are responsible for your life. You can't keep blaming somebody else for your dysfunction. Life is really about moving on."

You have already been failing a hundred times in your thinking already, so why bother taking the next step? And that's the key problem, which we need to address. It is not the actual failure you are facing; it is about all your thoughts of failure that happens to you every day.

In the later section of this book, we will talk about the way to mold your thinking and change the way you think about failure in the first place.

What Do You Think Will Happen If You Fail?

"The greatest mistake you can make in life is to continually be afraid you will make one." ~ Elbert Hubbard

You would agree by now that most of the fears in our lives are not real, rather these are all in the way we think and perceive the circumstances in our lives. By now, you had already noticed multiple types of reasons that make you think and feel afraid of impending fear.

But before we talk about how to change our relationship with fear and start looking at things, some more peeling is required. Before we jump towards discussing the strategies or tactics to overcome the fear of failure, it is better that we do some more introspection by digging deeper into our heads.

In this brief section, let's try to assess what exactly you think will happen to you if you fail in the real world. The idea behind this part of the book is to completely deconstruct this concept of failure knowing the origins of the fear of failure (which we already explored) and then also examining the worst-case scenario (which you will see in this section).

I will first try to capture what people think about the outcome of failure. It is generally like as if some catastrophic volcano will explode if you fail. Then I will try to give you my perspective on your situation as to what can happen in the real world.

So let's get straight into that now.

1. You think you will be labelled as failure.

You think that if you are not able to achieve success, then it is not that event that has failed, but you think that *you* are a failure.

The ideal scenario should be that if some event has failed, then it should not be repeated and should be done in a different way. But since you think that you are the failure, you determine that *you* are the problem and therefore you should not take any further action, once you fail.

It is a classic example of a fixed mindset, in which once you fail, you start to think that you are not made for that activity. You go one step further and convince yourself that there is no use of making any further effort. So you stop there. In my other book *The Mindset Makeover* I have categorically explained the different types of mindsets, including fixed and growth mindset in particular, which you will certainly find useful.

Had Edison adopted this kind of fixed mindset and belief system, he would not have attempted 999 wrong experiments before he could finally invent the lightbulb. At the first or second mistake or wrong experiment, he would have declared to himself that, "*I am a failure, so I should not keep trying.*"

Failure, of course, means that you have to label this activity as a failed activity or failed experiment. You think as if a tag with big bold words, "*I AM FAILURE*" is pasted on your forehead. So you are scared to look into the eyes of people or even at yourself, as you are fearful of realizing that the "failure tag" is pasted on your forehead. This imagination immediately prompts you to not take any further action, and you stop then and there.

But again, this is all in your head and the way you perceive failure in your life. It is not a reality, rather your imagination and personal perspective only.

Let's move to next one.

2. You think people will laugh at you.

Another horrible scene in your head—you think that people will laugh at you if you fail at anything. You start to imagine as if you are standing in the middle of a street and surrounded by people around you, who are making fun of you for having failed. Or you think that everyone working in your office is talking about you as a failure.

But this is not the case in reality. Everyone is busy in their own world. Everyone has their own problems, own struggles, and own daily challenges to earn a living. People even don't get time to spend with their families. Who's got the time to think about you? You are just a ten-second running wave of blurred memory in the minds of most people around you.

Okay, even assuming for a moment that people really have got the time to focus upon what you do, and they congregate at some place to point a finger at you and start making fun of you (I know, I am exaggerating here, but allow me to show you the other perspective, please), how much effect should it have on your life?

Compare for a moment the two different scenarios regarding a particular goal that would give you inner satisfaction and fulfillment.

Scenario 1—you are afraid of what people will think about you if you fail and don't try at all.

Scenario 2—you tried the thing which you wanted to achieve, but you failed, and now you are thinking that people are laughing at you (although you can't be completely sure if they are making fun of you or they are praising your courage).

In my view, out of two choices, regretting vs. failing, the latter will give you more fulfillment.

Don't worry too much about other people because:

"In the end, people will judge you anyway, so don't live your life impressing others, live your life impressing yourself." ~ Buddha

Okay, to show you a different perspective on this, let me ask you, how often do you think about your neighbor or your office colleague? How much interest do you have in his or her personal life or activities he or she pursues?

I have been long-plagued with the disease about people laughing or making fun of me. As I told in the first section of the book, I didn't release my book for weeks and then didn't say a word for weeks about the book even after publishing it. And the reason was that I thought, what would people think about me? They will make a fun of me for writing a personal development book after spending more than a decade and a half in a serious profession like "law." I even thought that a lawyer was one of most sought-after professions, so why would a lawyer want to become a writer?

At the same time, I see the people who have practiced successfully as lawyers for many years and then have turned into authors. People like Robin Sharma, Jonathan Fields, and John Grisham had all been in the legal profession before turning into authors. So, I thought, *why can't I be?*

I am exposing my true inner self to show you that everyone has some sort of inner reservations or fear. But you can only overcome those if you take action. Else how would you be ever able to find your true self? I took action, and within less than a year, I was showing up in the top 100 most popular authors in the business category. I am not boasting here (okay, maybe I am) but my purpose is primarily to show you the world of possibilities.

Similarly, you may have your inner desires or aspirations that you have hidden in your heart for years due to this false fear of people laughing at you, but my example should encourage you to try something from your heart.

I read somewhere that the older generation used to have a "lifer" kind of mentality, where they used to spend their whole life in one company. The previous generation has been much frequent in changing jobs—every three to five years. But this current generation has the thought of changing careers multiple times in their lives. I count myself as one of the examples of switching careers. And believe me, this is a pleasant journey so far, where you don't have Monday Blues, rather now you have "Sunday Blues," where taking a break seems to be delaying your reaching the top of the mountain.

One funny example I recalled out of Tim Ferriss's book, *The 4 Hour Work Week* suggested that to overcome the fear of what people will think about you, you should do something surprisingly crazy. He suggested things like, in the middle of an open cafeteria, suddenly lie down on your back and watch the reaction of the people around you. Of course, they will laugh at you and make fun of you. The idea is to get used to people making fun of you so that you don't have to be bothered by what people think about you. Though I personally would not be comfortable trying this.

Let's get to the next explosion, which you might think will happen if you failed.

3. You think you will lose your identity and confidence.

You think that if you fail, it will ruin your identity. And in that case, you will be looking at yourself differently, and also you think that the people around you will view you in a negative way.

After all, it takes one's life to develop some identity. If you have set up your image as a brilliant student, or as an employee always moving up on the corporate ladder, or you have considered yourself to be an amazing entrepreneur, then any failure or setback may seem to be an imminent dent on your image.

You find yourself so closely associated with that identity more than any others. In fact, the bigger problem is that you are so attached with that identity that any failure seems to be a life-threatening experience.

This problem is only due to your attaching too much importance to one of your identities. You remember the instance of a student scoring 96% (instead of 98%) and then committing suicide in the previous chapter. He took such a drastic step, only because in his mind he thought that he had lost his identity and therefore there is no point in living anymore.

Since you think that you will lose your identity once you fail in anything, you also worry about losing confidence in your domain. Therefore, to avoid losing your identity and thus losing your confidence, you tend to play small.

But this is not the right approach. Tony Robbins's quote below is the right advice here.

"Stay committed to your decisions, but stay flexible in your approach."

You failed because you wanted to test something that had the potential for you to reach your desired goals. If that experiment or approach fails, you should maintain a flexible attitude and keep exploring other avenues to reach your goal.

Stay tuned; you will find more actionable stuff in a later section of this book to overcome your fear of failure.

4. Your loved ones will be disappointed.

You also think that if you fail, your loved ones will be sad and disappointed. There are two ways of making them happy. Number one— just focus on your goal with discipline and perseverance and aim for achieving the goal which will make them happy. The other option is to avoid any failure and thus avoid making any mistakes—your loved ones may be happy, but in that case, you have already lowered your goals. Now this lowered goal doesn't demand much of you because, now instead of opting for running a marathon, you have given yourself the goal of just a one-mile race.

"It is impossible to live without failing at something unless you live so cautiously that you might as well not have lived at all—in which case, you fail by default." ~ J.K. Rowling

You note that this way, solely to avoid failure and thus to avoid the disappointment of your loved ones as a result, you don't aim for higher goals. Of course, you tell your loved ones that you have not failed, but on the other hand, in your heart, you know that you have reduced goal only due to your fear of failure, which is a failure in itself.

5. You will lose your money.

Failure in most cases also means losing your money. If you are to set up a business besides your day job, or if you are a stay at home parent and want to set up a source of income for you, of course you have to incur some initial costs.

Of course this risk will always be there. You can't gain anything if you are not willing to lose something. Let's try to understand this.

Why do you try to do different things?

Because you believe that such change will improve your life—this could be a small improvement (e.g. an additional $500 to $1000 in your monthly income) or a big improvement (e.g. a source of income that could replace your day job entirely).

But before you get there, you have to invest your time (which also has some cost associated with it) and some money to create something of value that people would pay you for.

I was reading that Amazon has spent billions of dollars, which they call "failure funds" on experimenting. Only from testing and experimenting, will they be able to come out with some unique idea, which can pay for all those costs.

"Failure and innovation are inseparable twins,"[ii] says Jeff Bezos, Amazon Founder.

"We all have that when we are little, but as we get older, somehow it's not as cool to fail," Bezos said. "It looks clumsy. So we get in our grooves. We have a set of expertise and skills. It's kind of a comfort zone. But you have to constantly push yourself and say, 'no, I don't care about failure.'"

"At Amazon, we have to grow the size of our failures as the size of our company grows," he said. "We have to make bigger and bigger failures—otherwise none of our failures will be needle-movers. It's a very bad sign over the long run if Amazon wasn't making larger and larger failures. If you do that all along the way, that is going to protect you from ever having to make that big hail mary bet that you sometimes see companies make right before they fail or go out of existence."

Similarly, venture capital funds know well in advance that out of every ten investments they make, eight to nine are going to fail. But they also know that the one or two investments, which eventually will succeed will be such

[ii] https://www.geekwire.com/2016/amazon-founder-jeff-bezos-offers-6-leadership-principles-change-mind-lot-embrace-failure-ditch-powerpoints/

huge that these will pay off the entire cost of the failed investments.

I am not suggesting that you should put your fortune or life savings at stake, but I am rather suggesting that you should make your calculation in advance and be ready to bear some risk of money because there are no guarantees in life.

In some cases, you could reduce the monetary expenditure by investing more of your time, i.e., instead of hiring people; you work yourself for some time.

Keep in mind that you are venturing into something that you anticipate will make your life better or even turn around your life. So if something has this kind of potential, then you have to be ready for bearing some risk.

Because, as is rightly said:

"The biggest risk a person can take is to do nothing." ~ Robert T. Kiyosaki

****

Part III: World's Most Famous Failures

12 of the World's Most Famous Failures—Who Persisted Long Enough

"All men dream, but not equally!

Those who dream in the dark recesses of the night awake in the day to find all was vanity.

But the dreamers of the day are dangerous men, for they may act their dreams with open eyes, and make it possible." By T.E. Lawrence

1. A Regular Teacher's Failure Story

This man was doing a simple job as an English teacher at a university in China for many years. In his childhood years, he failed a key primary school test twice. He was terrible in math and scored less than 1% in his math portion of his college entrance examination.

How does that sound? Anybody might think he was dumb, right? In fact, that's what we call the kids at school who somehow manage to score 50% on tests.

The failure story continues. He applied for 30 different kinds of jobs after he completed his schooling and graduation. No one selected him. He went to apply for police jobs. There were five job applicants including him. Guess what? The other four were selected for different positions, but he was rejected. When KFC entered China, he applied for a job at KFC. 24 people went for the job position, and again others got selected, but this young man got rejected again.

You must be realizing that this man had nerves of steel. Yes, he still carried on. He applied to Harvard University for higher education. He applied ten times for the education program—all ten times he was rejected or what you call might call, "failed." The journey continued one rejection after rejection, failure after failure.

Today, this man is worth approximately $39 billion and is Asia's richest man, according to Forbes[iii]. He is Jack Ma, the founder and executive chairman of Alibaba Group, a conglomerate of internet-based businesses.

In his own words in an interview with Charlie Rose[iv] in Davos, he stated, "I failed a key primary school test two times, I failed the middle school test three times, I failed the college entrance exam two times and when I graduated, I was rejected for most jobs I applied for out of college. I applied for Harvard ten times, got rejected ten times and I told myself that 'someday I should go teach there.'"

Jack Ma's perspective about failure is so visible in his quote, when he says, *"No matter what one does, regardless of failure or success, the experience is a form of success in itself."*

Jack Ma is a classic rags-to-riches story, but even more impressive than his fabulous wealth is his uncanny level of persistence. He is proof that no series of failures (despite how cripplingly depressing) can keep someone from achieving their dreams. As Jack Ma humbly notes, "I call Alibaba '1,001 mistakes'."

iii
https://www.forbes.com/sites/russellflannery/2017/08/20/alibabas-jack-ma-is-back-on-top-as-asias-richest-man/#5d46d3f14e75
iv https://www.investopedia.com/university/jack-ma-biography/

His quotes are so inspiring. Take one more from him: "*If you don't give up, you still have a chance. Giving up is the greatest failure.*"

It was intriguing to read in the news that the man who was rejected from jobs multiple times in his life recently had discussions with Donald Trump on how to create one million US jobs over the period of next five years. Isn't that worth applause?

The most important thing I take from this story is the relationship that he established with failure and the most resourceful perspective he chose to adopt for failure. While others tremble with fear of failure and don't move an inch, Jack Ma was always challenging his fear in all facets of life. The life he has created is not magic or sheer luck, but he laid a very strong foundation of a resilient mindset while facing the mindset.

There are tons of such examples of people who defeated failure by their persistence in the face of difficult times and perseverance by staying put in the game despite the fact that their success took longer. They used the formula:

"**Fail Fast Forward,**" meaning they kept on failing and continued to move forward until they tasted success.

Let's look at few more terrible failures.

2. A Basketball Player Failing Massively

Michael Jordan was removed from his high school basketball team because he was shorter than the minimum height for playing basketball. On that day, he went home and locked himself in his room and literally cried for hours. But he persisted and didn't give up.

Today, Michal Jordan is considered one of the best basketball players in the world. He already has many accolades in his name, like six times NBA champion, five times NBA Most Valuable Player, fourteen times NBA All-Star and many more[v].

He has always considered failure as a stepping stone to success. His famous quote below on its own explains how he perceived failures coming in his life.

"I have missed more than 9,000 shots in my career. I have lost almost 300 games. On 26 occasions I have been entrusted to take the game-winning shot, and I missed. I have failed over and over and over again in my life. And

[v] https://en.wikipedia.org/wiki/Michael_Jordan

that is why I succeed." ~ Michael Jordan

You can see from the words above that this man didn't consider failure as any stigma in his career. Rather, he has proudly stated all the failures of his life and ultimately given the whole credit of his success to his failures.

You can easily imagine the relationship that successful people maintain with failure. So when the failures come their way, such people know that this is a part of the whole growth trajectory—a necessary ingredient for the recipe for success.

If someone has deeply imbibed such a perspective about the failure, do you think such person would stop at any failure? Do you think that such a man would ever think of giving up or killing his or her dream or ambition? I don't think so.

They don't consider failure as opposite to success; rather they have a perspective that failure is an integral part of success.

3. A Failed Politician for Life

Look at this man's failures spread across his entire working life. He has failed in all areas of his work life, personal life, and health.

- 1816: His family was forced out of their home. He had to work to support them.

- 1818: His mother died.

- 1831: He failed in business.

- 1832: He ran for state legislature and lost.

- 1832: He lost his job and wanted to go to law school but couldn't get in.

- 1833: He borrowed some money from a friend to begin a business and by the end of the year, he was bankrupt. He spent the next seventeen years of his life paying off this debt.

- 1835: He was engaged to be married, but his sweetheart died, and he was heartbroken.

- 1836: He had a total nervous breakdown and was in bed for six months.

- 1838: He sought to become speaker of the state legislature and was defeated.

- 1840: He sought to become elector and was defeated.

- 1843: He ran for Congress and lost.

- 1846: He ran for Congress again. This time he won and went to Washington.

- 1848: He ran for re-election in Congress and lost.

- 1849: He sought after the job of land officer in his home state, but was rejected.

- 1854: He ran for Senate of the United States and lost.

- 1856: He sought the vice-presidential nomination at his party's national convention, but received fewer than 100 votes.

- 1858: He ran for U.S. Senate again and again he lost.

- 1860: He was elected the president of the United States.

You can't even imagine how one can survive so many failures and tragedies, but Abraham Lincoln reached the topmost position of the most developed nation in the world— president of United States, despite all this.

See the notable quotes from this legend:

"Success is going from failure to failure without losing enthusiasm."

"Always bear in mind that your own resolution to succeed is more important than any other thing."

Again, you can see the pattern from the lives of successful people. No successful person has ever treated failures, and even massive tragedies, as an excuse to move back. It requires a tremendous amount of work on your psychology and mindset to change your perception of failure. Once you start seeing failure as a necessary part for success (and yes, it is a fact—you won't see many successful people who have achieved that without any failures), then you will not be scared of failure and become unstoppable.

4. Poor Homeless Failure Turned Author

Who doesn't know the bestselling author of the world-famous Harry Potter Series, J. K. Rowling? She publicly acknowledged how big a failure she was during her entire life before she hit success through her Harry Potter series.

A few short years after her graduation from college, her worst nightmares were realized. In her words, "I had failed on an epic scale. An exceptionally short-lived marriage had imploded, and I was jobless, a lone parent, and as poor as it is possible to be in modern Britain, without being homeless. The fears that my parents had had for me, and that I had had for myself had both come to pass, and by every usual standard, I was the biggest failure I knew."

Currently, she has a net worth of $650 Million, according to Forbes's estimate. What a journey from an epic failure (in her own words) to an envious success story. But she has publicly acknowledged the importance of failure in her life, which has led her to this mega success. Below is what she stated about the significance of failure in her commencement speech at Harvard University[vi].

"It is impossible to live without failing at something unless you live so cautiously that you might as well not have lived at all—in which case, you fail by default.

[vi]

https://news.harvard.edu/gazette/story/2008/06/text-of-j-k-rowling-speech/

Failure gave me an inner security that I had never attained by passing examinations. Failure taught me things about myself that I could have learned no other way. I discovered that I had a strong will and more discipline than I had suspected; I also found out that I had friends whose value was truly above the price of rubies.

The knowledge that you have emerged wiser and stronger from setbacks means that you are, ever after, secure in your ability to survive. You will never truly know yourself, or the strength of your relationships until both have been tested by adversity. Such knowledge is a true gift, for all that it is painfully won, and it has been worth more than any qualification I ever earned."

You again see that these people maintain a different kind of relationship with fear of failure. We will get much deeper into how these people were able to deal with failure, not once or twice, but in some cases their entire lives, before they tasted success.

Let's continue to have a quick look at some more people, who traveled and failed massively on their path in their journey towards success.

5. Walt Disney

Mickey Mouse creator, Walt Disney, went bankrupt at the age of 22, after the brutal failure of his cartoon series. He also wanted to become a Hollywood actor, but it never happened. He is often quoted as fired from a newspaper for "lacking imagination" and "having no original ideas."

But finally, this creator of Mickey Mouse went on to be nominated for 59 Academy Awards, winning 22, all for his unparalleled animations. As a film producer, Disney holds the record for most Academy Awards[vii] earned by an individual.

"All the adversity I've had in my life, all my troubles and obstacles, have strengthened me... You may not realize it when it happens, but a kick in the teeth may be the best thing in the world for you." ~ Walt Disney

His quote above gives a clear indication of what his outlook was towards the failure. He was rather grateful that he encountered all these adversities and failures in life, which

---

vii https://en.wikipedia.org/wiki/Walt_Disney

helped him realize his worth and thus create his empire.

6. Albert Einstein

If someone asks to name a genius, most people will come up with the name Albert Einstein. Even for Einstein, the great scientist of our history and the father of modern physics, being a genius did not come easy.

He was known as slow in learning how to speak. His school headmaster told his mother that her child had below average intelligence and issued a note to that effect stating that he could not study in the school. The headmaster even expressed his view to her that Einstein would not amount to much in his life.

But later in his life, Einstein received a Ph.D. and was recognized as a leading theorist. A few years after that he won a Nobel Peace prize for physics and began to be recognized as the genius of our modern era.

In his words:

"Failure does not mean that you are a failure, it just means that you have not succeeded yet."

He also quoted:

"Anyone who has never made a mistake has never tried anything new."

Again, you see the common pattern in the lives of all successful people. They don't see failure as an evil or bad thing to avoid. Rather, each of them has taken failure as the learning ground and as a springboard towards higher achievement in life.

7. Bill Gates

The secret behind Bill Gates's success after Microsoft went public in 1986, and Bill Gates became a 31-year-old billionaire; he was asked what his secret was to his success.

Gates replied, "there's no secret. I worked really hard on my idea to get it as good as I could, and then knocked on door after door."

- I ended up showing my idea to 1,200 people.
- 900 said no.
- 300 people showed some interest.
- Only 85 people actually did anything.
- 30 took a serious look.
- And 11 made me a multi-millionaire.

99% of the people that Bill Gates showed his idea to rejected him.

So the secret to his success was rejection or failure. Had he been scared at the rejection he first faced after knocking on the first door, he would have certainly become a failure. You can see that to reach those eleven people who made his fortune, he had to reach out to 1,200 people. To try something more than a thousand times definitely requires a pragmatic approach towards life circumstances. Even though you have courage in your guts, you keep on failing or getting rejected numerous times. It is difficult to get up and still pursue the course. It is only possible when you change your perspective towards failure. If you start looking at the failure as a necessary ingredient towards your journey towards success, then it is only a matter of time until you succeed.

8. Thomas Edison

Thomas Edison, an American inventor and businessman, who has been described as America's greatest inventor, also was ridiculed in his childhood. A teacher told him he was "too stupid to learn anything," and this man has shown the light to the whole world through his intelligence.

You know how he has understood the definition of failure. You already know how many times he failed and how he looked at his failures. Look at his famous quotes:

"I have not failed. I've just found 10,000 ways that won't work."

"Our greatest weakness lies in giving up. The most certain way to succeed is always to try just one more time."

9. Steve Jobs

Most of us know that Apple started off with two men in a garage. Today, this brand is worth about $750 billion of market capitalization with over 100,000 employees, according to Forbes Report. Almost unbelievably, Steve Jobs, the founder of Apple, was fired from the very company he began. But Steve took a completely different lesson from this failure. This dismissal made him realize that his passion for his work exceeded the disappointment of failure. His further ventures such as NeXT and Pixar eventually led Jobs back to the CEO position at Apple.

"I didn't see it then, but it turned out that getting fired from Apple was the best thing

that could have ever happened to me," Steve
Jobs said in 2005.

You see another example of getting the most
impactful lessons from the adversities and
failures of life.

10. Colonel Sanders

Colonel Sanders had been quite a failure in
dozens of areas he tried for most of his
working life until his late fifties. His latest
business was selling chicken dishes at a
service station. One of the most amazing
aspects of his life is the fact that when he
reached the age of 65, after running a
restaurant for several years, Sanders found
himself penniless. He retired and received his
first social security check, which was for $105.
And that was just the starting point of his
international fame and financial success story.

His chicken recipe was rejected 1009 times
before anyone accepted it. Finally, Sander's
"secret recipe" was coined "Kentucky Fried
Chicken," and then it became a hit.

Don't you think this is the ultimate example of
staying persistent long enough to reach the
height of success at the age of 65 and to build

a global empire out of his fried chicken business?

11. Stephen King

Stephen King was working as a teacher in rural Maine when he wrote his first novel, *Carrie*. King had some small successes selling short stories previously, but nothing that anyone could create a "career" on.

King submitted *Carrie* thirty times. King was rejected thirty times. Before his thirty-first attempt, he threw the manuscript out. His wife rescued it and asked him to try one more time. The rest is history.

King has already written more than fifty fiction books on horror, suspense, science fiction, and fantasy and has sold more than 350 million copies of his books.

12. Steven Spielberg

Steven Spielberg is considered one of the founding pioneers of the New Hollywood era, as well as being viewed as one of the most popular directors and producers in film history.

He was rejected both times he applied to film school at University of Southern California

(USC). That didn't stop him. Spielberg has grossed $8.5 billion from films he directed. His net worth as indicated by Forbes is $3.6 billion.

The Message

As I have been emphasizing earlier, there is a central theme to all these failures to success stories.

All the successful people have developed a different kind of relationship with their fear of failure. They have remained persistent during the tough times with a great faith that things will work out. They have worked on making their mindset more resilient with each failure. Moreover, they have, in part, insulated themselves from any outside negative thoughts, which could hamper their journey.

In this section, we learned how these people dealt with their failures and turned turned them into successes. Understanding these patterns and common traits of successful people is very important for the reason very well explained by Tony Robbins in his quote below:

"Success leaves clues."

Now in the next chapter, we will do some introspection on what is your current definition of fear of failure and how you should redefine your relationship with failure.

So let's keep going.

****

Part IV: Rewire New Belief System & Change Your Definition of Failure

"Failure is a bruise, not a tattoo." ~ John Sinclair

In the initial sections, we examined which type of failure we should avoid and which fear is worth embracing. You also went deeper into your "What If I Fail?" syndrome to examine the source of your negative thinking and also what bad things, in your view, might happen in your life, if you fail in your attempt.

In the previous section, we heard the stories of super successful people in their chosen domains. You already noticed that if you go deeper into the psychological layers of these people and examine the number of failures preceding their success, not all was that great.

It was all filled with rejection, failure, and hours slogging through unrewarding work, which later rewarded them immensely to such an extent that only a fraction of 1% of people on this planet reach.

The question for the ages is how come there is such huge difference in the results achieved by these ultra-successful people, while others are living in a life of mediocrity? I have always been curious to examine those traits and have been reading about this topic for the last decade. I initially understood this *intellectually,* but lately, I am internalizing this feeling *experientially*.

In fact, it is not that hard to understand what brought success to these people. Anyone, sincerely looking for answers can find the secrets of success of these people. There are already a large number of great books out there all explaining these traits of successful people. But the real problem to be tackled is how to implement those habits and traits in our daily life to live the life like these legends. Books can educate you and inform you about the approach followed by others, and you can also succeed following the process. Unfortunately, though, they cannot lead you through the experience of fear, which these people faced while standing tall in front of such fears or rejection.

The first and foremost requirement is to understand the approach or outlook you have towards a particular problem to be addressed. Therefore, it is important to assess your internalized perception or belief about failure before we move ahead and start taking any steps towards correcting.

A few years ago, I read a book titled, *Go for No—Yes is the Destination, No is How You Get There* by Andrea Waltz, which is a gem for anyone particularly into marketing and the sales profession. The wisdom of this book can be applied and implemented to any other area of the life where you confront rejections or failure. There is one specific example stated in the book, which I often quote to people when talking about success and failure, which requires a total mindset shift. It goes like this:

The example assumes your daily target is to secure two product sales orders before you call it a day. Now, by experience, it is a fair estimation that for securing two sales of the product in a day, you have to approach at the least twenty people that day. Now there are two approaches taken by people.

Approach 1: Contact your prospective customers, and whenever you get two sales as your target for that day, your job is done and you are done for the day. Most people follow this.

Approach 2: Since two sales come from twenty approaches and therefore eighteen rejections, people of this category target eighteen rejections a day. It means that they don't stop at meeting the target of two sales per day. They make the target of eighteen rejections a day, regardless of whatever number of sales they have already done.

You see there is a difference between the two different extremes. These two sets of people have a *different definition* of failure. They *think and feel differently* about failure. These two sets of people have a *different relationship* with the failure.

Before we move forward, let's look at the definition of failure.

What is Failure?

According to the Merriam-Webster dictionary, failure means a lack of success. The logical assumption that follows is that you're only successful when you reach your end goal. Otherwise, you are a failure. This definition entirely disregards the process involved in reaching the success. It's spelled out in black or white terms: it's either success or a failure. This disempowering definition is one of the primary reasons why people fear failure because they think they will be labeled as a failure.

So, if you are considered a failure in this approach, there's no doubt that you would want to avoid failure at any cost.

But that's not the approach that successful people follow. They consider failure in an entirely different way—rather they use the emotion of fear of failure as fuel for success. After all, staying put even after so many rejections and failures does not happen on its own on a long-term sustainable basis. It needs a psychological shift—in your mindset.

Change Your Beliefs

The following are the necessary beliefs that one needs to engrave deeply in their head like a brain tattoo. You should believe these not merely because I am saying it and not merely because all the people who have believed them have succeeded. You should use these beliefs because the other way around is not at all supportive—you will simply keep dragging through your life, but there would be something in your heart which you will be longing for.

If you are happy with whatever you earn or with your career and growth, however, then this book is probably not for you. Keep it aside and just go for a relaxed walk around. But since you are reading this book so far, it means you definitely want a better life, and something is coming in between you and your better life.

What's that something? It is the *fear of failure.*

I can assume that you are here with me because you want to change your life and make some important decisions. In order to progress faster towards your goal, you want to minimize the effect of this hurdle called fear of failure.

So come on and get ready to replace your negative beliefs about fear of failure and embrace some different but powerful beliefs about failure.

1. Fear of failure is the beacon.

Probably some of you know it well, but you have yet to experience it. Still, let me try to explain it a bit.

Try to put some pressure on your memory and try to think about some instances when you suddenly found yourself caught by this fear of failure. How does the process work? Let's deconstruct it further.

Whenever fear of failure engulfs you, the first step before that was that you thought about something you wanted to achieve at that time. That something could be you thinking of going to your boss and asking for a raise. It could be preparing for competitive examination. It could be that you have an opportunity of speaking on the stage with hundreds of people sitting in your audience. It could be starting a side business along with your job, or it could be a mega and life-shattering decision to quit your full-time job and to start a new business altogether.

In all these cases, you had first desired certain things to achieve in the first place. To put it differently, you thought that you would have a better life if you achieve those goals. Of course, clearing that exam will enable you to be admitted to a good college or institution, or to be accepted for a good job. Speaking on stage will boost your confidence and help you establish your authority in your area of expertise. Starting a new business would help you taste the freedom of time, and you can also gain financial freedom if your business succeeds.

It means whenever the fear of failure arises from doing something new (except those life-threatening fears of jumping from a mountain), that means it is beaconing towards what you should be exploring and taking further steps towards that.

Ralph Waldo Emerson has rightly stated as well:

"What you are afraid to do is a clear indication of the next thing you need to do."

If there is no fear arising while doing something different, however, it means either you are already familiar with the situation, or it is already in your safety zone.

"If it doesn't scare you, you're probably not dreaming big enough." ~ *Tory Burch*

If you know that fear of failure is the beacon towards your ultimate dreams or goals, then why don't you simply go ahead and take the actions. What holds you back despite being intellectually aware?

What holds you back is your operating system called the mind. Your mind is designed in such a way that it wants to safeguard you against any kind of discomfort or uncertainty. Doing anything new would mean that you are going out in the field of the unfamiliar, which will entail some element of uncertainty or insecurity in some manner to you. You would feel uncomfortable in doing that because you don't have experience of doing those things. Therefore, the mind will come in to safeguard you to avoid getting into any kind of risk. Why? Because your mind is designed to ensure your safety and survival. Any kind of new thing would appear to your mind as a danger, which in the first instance would do the job of alerting you and prompting you to stay safe (thanks to the amygdala in your brain, which we talked about in the previous chapter).

How do successful people handle this?

In fact, what they do is to *give more attention to the 'beacon'* and *less attention to the fictitious or imaginary obstacles* on the path towards their dreams. It doesn't mean that they don't ever think about the problems coming their way, but they think in a way that their goal is the ultimate object to be achieved, and whatever comes in the way, they consider that as a project to be handled. They don't treat the obstacles as problems, rather they assume that they are projects to be completed.

Therefore, assuming the fear as a beacon to something big is the first and foremost mindset shift needed for converting your fear of failure into fuel for success.

2. Failure is not permanent.

No one wants failure. In fact, everyone wants success in the first instance. But, except in rare cases, it is almost always a roller-coaster ride. One has to undergo physical, mental, and emotional turmoil before he achieves anything significant. But what allows successful people to achieve their goals is their understanding and belief that failure is temporary in nature. They understand that no matter how dark the night is, it will be over once the sun is out.

Only with this perspective is it possible to stay persistent and resilient after each failure. Abraham Lincoln wouldn't have become the president of United States if not for the number of failures he had seen in his life. You wouldn't have tasted the KFC chicken had Colonel Sanders not approached a thousand people to taste his 'chicken recipe,' despite facing rejection one after another. Bill Gates wouldn't have approached 1,200 people to give a demonstration of his Windows software if he had not believed that failure is temporary.

As Napoleon Hill has rightly stated:

"Remember when your plans fail, that temporary defeat is not permanent failure."

History is filled with examples, and you have already seen the most famous failures so far, who have persisted enough to succeed.

3. Failure isn't always too bad to handle.

Successful people believe that in whatever form the failure comes, it would never be so bad that it can't be handled. So they don't get unnecessarily fearful of what will happen if they fail. They are of the belief that whatever happens, they can start again.

Many successful people have filed bankruptcy in their businesses and have gained their fortune back. They keep moving forward on the belief that whatever happens, they will somehow manage to do.

"Don't cross the bridge, until it comes to you." ~ Proverb

There's a study that proves that most of the fears you keep in your mind don't happen. In this study, subjects were asked to write down their worries over an extended period and then identify which of their imagined misfortunes did not happen. It turns out that 85%[viii] of what subjects worried about

---

[viii] https://www.huffingtonpost.com/don-joseph-goewey-/85-of-what-we-worry-about_b_8028368.html

never happened, and with the 15% that did happen, 79% of subjects discovered either they could handle the difficulty better than expected, or the difficulty taught them a lesson worth learning. This means that 97% of what you worry about is not much more than a fearful mind punishing you with exaggerations and misperceptions.

4. Failure is the necessary element of the game.

Successful people believe that failure is like navigating a maze. If you imagine the process of working on your goal as navigating a maze, each failure teaches you what doesn't work. One by one, you're eliminating ineffective approaches. When you adopt this metaphor, failure won't mean the end. It will mean a new beginning.

Once you have that mindset that failing is just pruning out the wrong ways to work, then you are more focused on trying a different approach. You don't get stuck and start blaming the whole world as if it has conspired to make you fail.

If you look at the previous section on the world's most famous failures, you will notice that everyone has crossed the maze of failure multiple times in their life. Every quote from most of the successful people gives this message loud and clear that failure is the necessary element on your journey towards success. I can't emphasize the importance of failure anymore as Edison has quoted:

"I have not failed. I've just found 10,000 ways that won't work."~ Edison

5. The fear of failure and failure itself builds your character.

"Most great people have attained their greatest success just one step beyond their greatest failure."~ Napoleon Hill

Think about a broke person who wins the lottery and becomes an ultra-rich person in a short period. There are enough examples when people who have won the lottery become broke within few years.

Why is this so?

Because they have not gone through the pains of failure and obstacles coming in their way towards success. Success was placed in front of them in a well-served and decorated plate, and they simply had to eat it. But they couldn't digest the success because they couldn't develop that character that is needed to retain the success.

But look at Donald Trump. He reached the height of success, then he went bankrupt number of times, but he again was able to set up his whole empire again.

You might be already aware that Donald Trump has many failures[ix] accredited to his name. His first company, Trump Airlines, which is credited to bring luxury to people never made profits. It suffered huge losses and was finally shut down. His other failed ventures included Trump–the Board Game (on the same lines as Monopoly), Trump Casinos, Trump Mortgages, Trump University, Trump Magazine, and Trump Vodka all failed and subsequently shut down. But Trump earned his success from all the failures of his life. So this man has attained massive success under heavy weights of failures—and the ultimate success is occupying the most coveted position in the world being president of United States of America If success does always follow failure, Trump is a living example of that.

His mantra can be found in the quote below:

"What separates the winners from the losers is how a person reacts to each

---

[ix] https://successstory.com/inspiration/donald-trump-success-through-failures

new twist of fate." ~ *Donald John Trump*

Also, Randy Pausch quote aptly fits here:

"The brick walls are there for a reason. The brick walls are not there to keep us out. The brick walls are there to give us a chance to show how badly we want something."

6. Switch your thinking from "What if I fail?" to "What if I succeed?"

One of the key distinguishing factors between successful and mediocre people is the way they focus on empowering questions and invite the right amount of energy into their daily actions.

Imagine one person simply asking himself the question, "What if I fail" and then imagining being on the road with no means of earning, his house being claimed by the mortgage company, and other bad things happening to him.

When this person was engulfed by the negative thinking, the success-oriented person is asking a different set of questions. This person will get into an empowering state of mind by imagining what will happen to him if he succeeds on his project. He imagines himself filling with a sense of fulfillment by achieving the success and overcoming all struggles. He imagines the financial gains, the respect he would receive from society, the benefits his family will get from his success, and many other positive things coming to his life.

As you know, it takes a shift in your mindset and a focus on a different set of questions—empowering questions. Tony Robbins has rightly stated the importance of better life questions as below:

"Quality questions create a quality life. Successful people ask better questions, and as a result, they get better answers." ~ Tony Robbins

You would have realized by now that it is all about feeding your mindset with the right set of beliefs and soon you will start seeing the blue ocean of possibilities. We are all full of potential, and each of us is uniquely gifted by God to deliver value on this earth.

We will end this section with an inspirational extract from Marianne Williamson's book titled *A Return To Love: Reflections on the Principles of A Course in Miracles*, which aptly narrates the potential and vastness of human potential.

"Our deepest fear is not that we are inadequate. Our deepest fear is that we are powerful beyond measure. It is our light, not our darkness that most frightens us. We ask ourselves, Who am I to be brilliant, gorgeous, talented, fabulous? Actually, who are you not to be? You are a child of God. Your playing small does not serve the world. There is nothing enlightened about shrinking so that other people won't feel insecure around you. We are all meant to shine, as children do. We were born to make manifest the glory of God that is within us. It's not just in some of us; it's in everyone. And as we let our own light shine, we unconsciously give other people permission to do the same. As we are liberated from our own fear, our presence automatically liberates others." ~ Marianne Williamson

****

Part V: Proven Ways to Turn Your Fear of Failure into Fuel for Success

"Inaction breeds doubt and fear. Action breeds confidence and courage. If you want to conquer fear, do not sit home and think about it. Go out and get busy." ~ Dale Carnegie

I came across an acronym for this four-letter "F" word. Don't get me wrong, I am still on the subject and talking about this four letter word, "FEAR." It goes like this:

Face
Everything
And
Rise

Whoever has changed this dreaded word, "fear" into an empowering acronym has done a wonderful job. In fact, fear can be compared with darkness.

How can one overcome darkness? Someone can say, "I will conquer the darkness," but how would one do it? Darkness does not have its separate entity. Howsoever hard you try, you can't win over something that doesn't have its own separate entity. Darkness is just the absence of light.

Any sane person would tell that merely lighting a candle is sufficient to win over darkness. There is no big mystery behind this. I know you would say that this is so simple and obvious, but the irony is that we don't understand that this metaphor applies when we want to overcome our fears. Our actions taken in those moments of fear bring the light of courage to the darkness of fear.

You may say, "but I don't know what action to take." I will ask you: what would you do if you see a snake just a a hundred meters away coming towards you?

You have three choices:

    a. You could start running to reach a safer place. Maybe you get into your vehicle and drive at a speed of hundred miles an hour to escape from the snake.

b. You could wait for the snake to come to you and charm the snake if you are a snake charmer.
c. You could freeze with fear and hope that the snake just silently passes by you.

Most people would say the only first two choices are the wise choices. In the first one, you took the prudent action to escape and save your life, because you know you cannot fight with a snake. In the second case, your skillset is such that you can encounter a snake and catch hold of him. But in the third option, you decide not to take any action and just hope that everything would turn out okay on its own. What do you get out of this example?

The lesson is that, if you have got some urgency or priority, you always have some kind of choice in front of you to take. Once you have taken the first step, only that first action itself shows the light to take further actions. Let's try to understand this better with one more example.

Assume you are driving at a night on a lonely road with no lights on the road in some mountain area. You can only see around two-hundred meters away from your car's headlights, but you don't put an excuse that you don't have visibility of the full road so you won't drive. You start your car and begin your journey. You see, on the faith of visibility of just two-hundred meters away, you still travel a hundred miles during the night.

The same principle applies to your decisions in life. You don't need to know everything before you start. You don't need to fear the lack of information. You simply have to start with something, which is your best judgement at that particular time. It is all about taking at least some action despite your fears.

Moreover, all the decisions in life are not like the poisonous snakes sitting in front of you. Situations in life are never so fearful that you are not able to think of a next action to face the obstacles. Rather, in most situations, you create stories around your circumstances, which may feel like a life-threatening snake coming towards you or a tiger about to jump on you.

For example, you might see your boss shouting at you, like a ferocious tiger that might kill you. But in reality, it is not going to happen. Of course, not physically—so your life is safe. You could say, though, that he might fire you from the job, which in your view is as good as killing you. In my view, if you are genuinely doing your work in a diligent manner and delivering your best value to the organization, why would you be scared of your boss? If he or she has ulterior motives, then it is a different story. In that case, you may want to think about changing your department or job itself. Moreover, I don't think that your destiny is controlled by your boss or any other human besides yourself. It was a generation back when people used to spend a lifetime in a single organization. Today, the majority of the workforce changes jobs every three to five years. Therefore, if despite you being sincerely and diligently working on your deliverables, your superior is criticizing or finding fault in your work for no reasons, you should not get too worried. You just keep doing your job and keep exploring, and the chances are that in a short time, you would be able to secure another job outside the organization.

On the contrary, being scared or fearful and not taking any action would cost you, in terms of your behavior, performance, and deliverables, as compared to you taking at least some action in the direction of your fear. The double whammy is that this will give your boss more reasons to scream at you.

So why would you avoid taking action due to fear of failure? That's why David J. Schwartz has rightly said,

"Action cures fear. Indecision, postponement, on the other hand, fuel fear."

That is the straight-forward answer to your question about what to do when you are facing fear: take action, any action.

Instead of your forcing action, can your action pull you towards it?

So you know that you need to take action, but it might seem like you have to force the action upon you and do it. How would you feel if there is something that makes the process of taking action smoother and not strenuous? In other words, instead of you pushing yourself hard by taking action towards the objective you fear, there is something which pulls you to take action towards that particular goal. That's possible, but it would require a huge mindset shift, and that's the purpose of this section of this book.

In this section, you will learn the proven techniques and tactics, which will help you to control and overcome your fears. You have to put some time and work into it first, but I assure you that you will reap the major rewards soon. You will seemingly get so into an auto-pilot mode while taking action in front of fears that it would feel like you are riding a swing and enjoying the autonomous flow of things around you.

I believe now you are ready with all the psychological explanation of how the fear of failure works and how you need to adopt a different perspective towards failure, So let's jump straight into the actionable and effective strategies now.

Here you go...

1. Assess Your Real Motivation to Trigger Pull Effect

"Success demands singleness of purpose" ~ Vince Lombardi

As you have already learned in the previous section, fear is, in fact, a beacon towards what you want to achieve in your life. You are fearful of the things or events because it makes you feel like you will lose a lot if you fail.

If your goal is not to climb Mount Everest or swim across the Panama Canal, then you won't feel the fear of failure because you don't want to achieve that goal. You don't want to be see yourself waving your country's flag on Mount Everest. You don't want to see other people wave to you on the other side of the Panama Canal. Since you are not a participant in that game, you really don't bother about that. You won't ever feel like a failure, who couldn't climb the mountain or swim across the river. Rather you would avoid the mountains or rivers and forget about failing. You may definitely have a fear of dying from falling or drowning if you're ever accidentally trapped in such a situation, but you would never have a fear of failing in these activities. Why? Because you don't want that thing in the first place.

You only fear about the things you want

If you want to pass that coveted examination, which will help you to get admissions into a top engineering or management institution, you will be scared of the feeling of failure while preparing for that. Since you want to achieve success, and only because of this reason, you feel the fear of failure here. You want that dream job at your favorite company, so you fear of failing an interview. You want that handsome guy or gorgeous girl to say yes to your proposal to marry you, so you get a feeling of failure in your head.

You may think of any other example in your life and in your dreams, and you will reach the only conclusion that the fear of failure is only present when you want something. Period.

Now having established that fear of failure arises only when you have goals or milestones you want to achieve, the next most important question is *how do I eradicate that fear of failure from life*?

Hang on! I would still say you are jumping ahead of the gun. Before you even reach that point, you need to ask yourself, *do you really want that thing or it a fleeting desire*?

How badly do you still want it?

Ask yourself a few questions like this:

- Would I be able to forget about this goal easily, if I am busy or occupied in something else?
- If not, what exactly is my deepest motivation for fulfilling this dream?
  - Is it my personal life?
  - Is it something that I want to do for my parents, sibling, spouse or children, or friend?
  - Is it something that is a selfless goal (e.g., nurturing underprivileged children, helping people affected by natural calamities)?
- Lastly, do I want it badly enough or will I forget about it tomorrow?

Why are the above questions so important?

It is because and I have personally tested that actions don't work that well until there is some inner drive to do it. If you have read my other books (you may check them out at www.sombathla.com), you would have noticed that I strongly emphasize the importance of working and improving your psychology first. It is the power of my psychological driving factors that are pulling me to create personal growth books at a faster pace. And at this juncture, I would be honest to tell you that writing these books are helping me equally as these are helping my readers. I convinced myself psychologically that I want to deeply understand all kinds of human emotions, both positive and negative. I am committed to exploring the possibility of human potential by reading more and more literature and implementing in my life and then conveying my message to the world.

So coming back to you, my dear reader (I truly care about you too with a deep love and respect), don't ever underestimate the importance of psychology behind why you do what you do. As Tony Robbins rightly states:

"Remember, the immutable law of life: 80% of success in life is psychology, and 20% is mechanics."

It is only deep self-motivation that makes things easier for you. Then you don't need to talk about any strategies to overcome fear.

Can you ask a mother how she will overcome the fear of being burned in a fire if her child is stuck in a fire? You know she has deeper than the deepest motivation—she is committed to save her child. So all the questions on how to overcome the fear of failure becomes redundant.

Before you get into the question of how you would conquer your fear, you have to ask yourself, *how badly do I want it*? I am restating one of the stories that you might have read in one of my other books that will put across the point clearly.

Let me tell you a brief story here first.

There was a monk in a village, and he became famous in his surrounding areas due to his teachings about how to live a great life. He was living a blissful life, and people used to come to him for blessings and for finding solutions to their problems. A very rich, but unhappy, person heard about this monk.

He thought that the monk must have the solution to his problem, so he went to meet this monk. He asked the monk, "I have everything in life, (i.e., money, name, fame, family, social status, etc.), but I am still finding my true calling, which is what gives me real fulfillment. I am not able to find it, and I don't know how to attain peace and state of fulfillment, which I now see on your face."

The monk listened patiently and then asked the rich man to follow him into his backyard. There was a small pond in the backyard. The monk told the man to get inside the pond, and then he would give the man answers to his deep questions.

The rich man hesitated, but still went inside. The monk sat outside on the bank of the pond. As soon as the rich man entered the pond, the monk held his head and forced his head under the water. The man started choking. The more force he applied to get out of the water, the monk pushed him more into the water. Finally, the rich man put his best shot forward and was able to get out of the grip of the monk to come out of the water.

He was furious and almost out of breath. So out of anger, he shouted at the monk, "You wanted to kill me or what? How do you think such action was necessary to give answers to my questions."

The monk said in a very compassionate way, "No, I didn't want to kill you, rather I wanted to see what you would do when you need oxygen to save your life." The rich man said obviously, "one would do anything when it comes to saving one's life."

The Monk smiled and told the man, "Yes, you have given the answers yourself."

"When you want wisdom and insight as badly as you want to breathe, it is then you shall have it."~ Socrates

So the answer to your quest is:

Until you want something so badly, like you want oxygen for your life, you won't be putting your best foot forward. And without that best shot, there is no way that you can get what you want.

You would always be in two boats. You think that you want to achieve this, but with any minor obstacle coming your way, you start thinking that the *status quo* (present state) is a better. You start justifying yourself by saying that, "A known devil is better than an unknown angel."

If you don't know, there are three different types of motivators: extrinsic, intrinsic, and prosocial.

a. Extrinsic motivators are about external rewards such as status, money, or praise. They're the weakest type of motivation.
b. Intrinsic motivators are about internal rewards: growth, challenge, enjoyment, or freedom.
c. Prosocial motivation is defined as the desire to expend effort to benefit other people.

Intrinsic and prosocial motivators are the most powerful and durable types of motivators. Why? Because they are emanating more from your deeper and inner desires. They are your true whys.

Therefore, if you really and badly want something deeply motivated by your intrinsic and prosocial motivators, then you are pulled by your goals, and you don't need to push through your emotions.

Okay, let's move on to the next one

****

2. Acknowledge Your Fears and Get Rid of Them

"Forget about the consequences of failure. Failure is only a temporary change in direction to set you straight for your next success."~ Denis Waitley

As you already know, that fear element is installed in your brain through a specific portion called the amygdala for necessary reasons—to ensure your very survival and to protect you from dangers.

Also, we already know that all fears are not bad. Some fears are healthy fears, and some fears can be unhealthy. Fear of falling from a big height keeps you maintain a safer distance. Any fear, which is there for your survival is a good fear.

Now, even this fear of falling from big height takes the shape of an adventure. Yes, even a fall from 12,000 feet in the air to the ground can be a thrilling and adventurous experience worth taking, if you do a bungee jumping from an airplane. I don't need to explain the difference here. You already see that if you are going ahead with a trained adventure specialists to give you an out-of-this-world experience, there should not be fear rather a sense of achievement.

Falling from a mountain, unless you are an adventurer or mountaineer, is a real fear, which you must respect and take all precautionary actions to safeguard yourself. On the other hand, falling from a bungee jump should not be fearful, rather it should be an adrenaline rush experience for you. Our role should be to respect the healthy fears and remove the unhealthy fears from the runway of our life, so we can increase the pace of our airplane to touch the sky.

I urge you to imagine what kind of emotions you have experienced in your heart and body when you thought of these two different scenarios. I will explain to you in a bit why we are doing all these exercises shortly in this section, but for a moment try to remember those experiences in your body, mind, and heart.

Now, think about a dream you want to achieve, but are scared of failing in that. You don't need to apply much pressure on your mind because dreams always keep floating in your heads, though mostly clouded under our emotions of fear.

Okay, have you thought about your dream yet? It could be you acing an examination for your future, it could be an interview for your next dream job, it could be your side-hustle business towards attaining freedom from a 9-to-5 cubicle job, or it could be leaving everything aside and jumping to start your own business. Anything that is close to your heart!

Now, where we fail to differentiate in our lives is the nature of our fear. Is it real or is it only imaginary? Is it a healthy fear or an unhealthy fear?

If someone is emotionally attached to these dreams, then failure to attain the dream can be devastating. In other words, if you don't get admission to Harvard, or you don't get a job at Google or Apple, you will feel heartbroken. It is so tragic to see that some people are so emotionally attached to their dreams that they literally end their life once they fail in that (remember the example in the previous section about someone committing suicide for not securing 98% in exams). But I know you are nowhere near that, because you are taking action and looking for solutions to these problems and reading this book as an action to conquer your fears.

So coming to my point, these failures are not the end of your life. It won't be like falling from a mountain and dying. Rather, it would be like an adventure ride. It will evolve you emotionally as well as physically and psychologically, once you cross that journey.

Remember, you are not alone in feeling like this. Every single human being on the planet experiences fears from time to time. There is simply no way of getting around this! Remember what you resist, persists. So you don't need to try to push your fear away. You just need to shift your relationship with your fear.

Highly successful people, for example, have learned how to say "hello" to their fear when it comes up and to keep taking the actions they know they need to take regardless. Think of something you'd love to be, do, or have that is not currently in your experience.

Would you like to be earning more money? Would you love to find your soulmate? Or transform your current relationship? Or perhaps start your dream business, or write a book?

To create a result you don't currently have, you're going to have to be willing to do something you've never done. You're going to have to be willing to take action that may feel scary, but you know will bring you closer to something that's in alignment with your highest good. So when you know there's an action for you to take that will move you toward transforming one of your dreams and desires into reality, then fear, doubt, or worry will almost always arise.

1. Acknowledge that you feel afraid. Say to yourself, *"Ok, I feel afraid right now. I'm going to stop and take a few deep breaths and re-center myself."*

2. Tell your fear, *"Thank you for stopping by, take a seat! But there's something I have to do before I can visit with you."*

3. Then, make a note on your calendar as to when you will make time to revisit and entertain that fear. Then, go ahead and take the action that there is to take toward your dreams and desires! Chances are after you've taken that action, when it's time to keep that appointment with your fear, the two of you probably won't have much to talk about.

As is rightly said:

"Feel the fear and do it anyway." ~ **Susan Jeffers**

****

3. Take Responsibility for Your Dreams—No One Else Will!

"Some people die at 25 and aren't buried until 75." ~ Benjamin Franklin

Okay, let's try to understand where dreams come from. Do you generate them on your own? No, I don't think it is so. So from where they come from?

Have you ever tried to understand some other aspects of our human body and mind? From where does the breath come from? Where does hunger come from? No, none of these activities are controlled by us. These are involuntary acts. We eat, drink, sleep, and clean our bodies—all these are a natural process, so nothing is in our control.

In a way, there is no difference between any animal on this earth and the human being. They do the same things. Your dog or cat or any other animal also does the bodily activities, like breathing, eating, sleeping, etc.

But, there is one huge difference between animals and human beings. While animals have a brain that functions to control all the bodily activities and ensure their survival, its role stops there only. But human beings have additionally been given with the precious gift of consciousness and thinking, which makes us uniquely capable of thinking.

So the dreams come from this unique ability of human beings to think and think so hugely to even cross the boundaries of countries and planets. It is only the human being in this universe who can think, and no other living creatures are equipped with that. Why do you think that such a distinctive ability given to you should be used to do only such activities that other animals can also do very comfortably?

Because you have the potential to create anything you can imagine. You know it already. And you won't be the first one to start to dream. Your fellow Homo sapiens have already taken the huge ride in this universe to fulfill their dreams and already to live a life full of dreams.

Why do only human beings strive for more and more? It is because the whole human journey is a journey of evolution—the journey of finding yourself. I am not getting into spirituality here, but the human drive to obtain more and more on this planet and then to reach to the other planet is nothing but an internal desire to be the whole (or merge with the whole). You always strive for more and more to be happy, so your journey is for the ultimate big.

The above may sound like a spiritual aspect of life, but I was trying to show you the bigger picture. Okay, let me get you back to this material world again. So, I was trying to lead you to a conclusion that your birth as a human being is not solely to make ends meet. You see that people manage to earn their bread somehow if they are willing to put something into action. That is not so difficult to do. God has not sent you on this planet to starve. If he has created a hunger in your body, then simultaneously, He has given your mind to think, eyes to see, feet to walk, and hands to do the work, which can help you earn your share of food on this earth. So at least there's no need to worry about basic survival.

Rather, your worry should be about the bigger potential, which a human being is born with that should not go waste. A seed never knows that it can turn into a big banyan tree. If you could ever talk to a younger seed and tell it that it has the potential to become a banyan tree, maybe it will laugh at you. Imagine a small seed laughing at you and saying, "Come on, you are joking. How can I be such a big tree?" But when this seed is laughing at you, you might be pitying it or sympathizing that this seed is so unaware of its potential.

The only factor is that out of maybe a thousand seeds, only one seed will have that potential. But there is no way to guarantee which one seed will become a banyan tree. You don't know, which seed has the stamina to handle all the sunlight, heat, water, and air and then blossom into the small plant and then turn into a big tree.

Similarly, if you imagine yourself as a seed, which has the potential to turn into a giant tree, then you might have similar doubts about yourself. Who knows if you are going to be the next Nobel Peace Prize winner, or the next Booker prize grabber, or the next sports superstar, or the next top-notch professional in your area. You might laugh at my arguments like the younger seed was laughing at you when you told him about his potential.

As Benjamin Franklin rightly stated:

"You can do anything you set your mind to."

Same is true with thousands of sperms trying to fuse with an egg. No sperm knows which one will be able to produce a human life. Likewise, no one knows that his or her life could be like that of Einstein, Mother Teresa, Nelson Mandela, Richard Branson, or Elon Musk. Who knows?

Even you don't know unless you experiment. You have the potential to know what you are destined to become. But the first step starts only after you overcome the fear of failure in your journey towards your goals. You need to turn your fear of failure into a mechanism of testing what you are made for. You need to put yourself into action like a seed before you can ever think of achieving your dream.

In fact, there is a much bigger question than, "*What if I fail?*" which stops you at the very first place, as if any failure will lead to an end of your life. The much bigger question is:

"What if I am not able to live my dreams?"

That is the real frustration of life. When you are at the end of your life, the only regret you will feel is the regret of not trying to take actions towards your dreams.

So, consider your dream as your asset. Your dreams are your net worth. The bigger the dreams, the more massive the action is required of you. If you only think of just scraping by day by day, it won't prompt you to take any action.

"If you don't build your dreams, someone else will hire you to help them build theirs." ~ Dhirubhai Ambani

This section of the book is written specifically to change the direction of your questions from your fear of failure to the significance of your dreams as a human being. You need to bring a psychological shift in your mindset before you can ever think of implementing any strategies or tactics. Implementing the tactics is only like cleaning the leaves of the trees from outside to keep them shining, whereas making a shift in your psychology is like watering the plant. So, it's better to work on your mindset first.

Fulfilling your dreams is only your responsibility and nobody else's. You have the potential to attain anything, provided that you focus on what you want out of your life and not get distracted by the short-term failures or struggles along the way. You need to change the direction of your focus on more empowering thoughts, and soon you will be attracting the right resources and the right people to get you going.

That's why it is rightly said:

***"Where focus goes, energy flows. And if you don't take the time to focus on what matters, then you are living a life of someone else's design."*~ Tony Robbins**

****

4. Use This Five Letter "F-Word" to Overpower Your Fears

"I believe if you keep your faith, you keep your trust, you keep the right attitude, if you're grateful, you'll see God open up new doors." ~Joel Osteen

What is the five-letter "F-Word" that you can use to kill this dreaded four-letter "F-Word" called Fear?

It is "Faith."

It is true from a simple mathematics perspective, right? Five letters is more than four, so should be more powerful as well. So let's first understand what exactly is Faith.

Merriam-Webster Dictionary defines the word faith[x] as the *"firm belief in something for which there is no proof"* or *"something that is believed especially with strong conviction."*

The world's top-most strategic coach, Tony Robbins puts it differently as the "certainty of outcome" in your mind before you start working on any of your goals. He states that

---

[x] https://www.merriam-webster.com/dictionary/faith

128

our success in any venture we get into entirely depends on the level of certainty of outcome in our minds. Because only our thinking about the certainty of outcome will trigger us to produce the quality of actions needed to get the results.

Take any example from your life, when you would have succeeded in something. Some of you might say that you don't consider having succeeded in something significant enough. I urge you to still think about any area of your life, however small, that you have succeeded in. It could be big or small.

For example, let's say you consider getting your current job as a success. Try to recollect the emotions when you were preparing for the job interview or when you were waiting outside for your turn for the interview. Of course, you might have some kind of nervousness, but there must have been a level of *certainty of outcome* in your mind that you will secure that job for you. Why I am so sure about that? Because your actions would have been entirely governed by that faith about your positive future that you are going to get that job.

You can easily compare the above example with any other instance in your life when you were not so sure of a positive outcome. You would realize that most of the things that you are not sure of achieving in life generally don't happen to you. The clear reason is that you don't put the necessary actions to achieve that goal.

So faith is the starting point before anything else in your journey towards your dreams.

"Faith is taking the first step even when you don't see the whole staircase." ~ Martin Luther King, Jr.

Despite your fear, if you choose to have faith or certainty of outcome in your mind, then your fear starts diminishing. The relationship between faith and fear is like a seesaw. When one is up, the other is down. So when we allow fear to rise, our faith will decline. But the opposite is true as well. When we increase our faith, our fear will fall.

Our scripture also narrate the importance of faith while dealing with fear.

"I prayed to the Lord, and He answered me, freeing me from all my fears." (Psalm 34:4)

Also, in the Gospel of Matthew[xi] 8, the disciple of Jesus had an experience with the

---

[xi]

https://www.biblestudytools.com/matthew/8.html

treacherous sea storm. Even though they had Jesus at their side, they let their circumstances drive their fear. As a life-threatening storm set in suddenly, not only did the disciples face the dangers of the rough waters, but they were surrounded by darkness as well. There were no life jackets. There were no lifeboats. They felt they were at the mercy of the great storm.

In a panic, they cried to Jesus, "Lord, save us! We're going to drown!" As Jesus woke from His sleep, He did not instantly calm the storm. Instead, He asked the disciples, "You of little faith, why are you so afraid?" Only after His rebuke did He calm the wind and waves. When Jesus spoke to the disciples, He acknowledged that their fears were great and their faith was little.

Many times, we want God to fix our problems instantly. We want the raging waters around us to cease immediately. Sometimes in the middle of the crashing waves, God has a word for us. He wants us to deepen our faith in Him before He intervenes. He wants us to follow in faith no matter how dark our circumstances seem.

How can you develop faith?

It is a matter of practice. It is just like asking how to have a healthy body. The answer is simple, and everybody knows it. You have to feed yourself well and exercise well. Similarly, developing faith is like building your mental health. Fear is the ailment for your mind, and in order to get a healthy mind, you need to feed it with a healthy dose of faith. Faith comes by instilling positive thoughts in your head more than the negativity, which either creeps in or you allow it to enter into your head.

The more you associate yourself with positive thinking and act upon the lessons learned, the more you will develop your faith muscle. There are multiple ways to utilize your time instead of allowing your mind to digress into fear-generating thoughts. You can read great literature on personal growth, associate with positive people, listen to free podcasts, watch free YouTube channels to immerse yourself in learning. But don't forget to implement the lessons in your life as quickly as possible; else all learning will just remain theoretical without real benefits.

One great podcast I can recommend is *Fear Not* by Billy Atwell from www.livingbeyondyourfears.com. I have also been a guest on his show, and you may listen to my story about how I overcame my fear of failure in that podcast. Podcast with my interview will be on air probably in early 2018.

The action you take based on faith will show you the way, and an action consistently taken will kill your all fears of failure.

"Faith leads to action; action leads to success." ~ Jacob Salem

****

5. Calm Your Mind & Receive Action Signals

"Go within every day and find the inner strength so that the world will not blow your candle." ~ Katherine Dunham

You already know that we are not talking here about any fear. We are talking about the fear that is real and fatal. The fear of failure we are talking about is an unhealthy kind of fear, which is all a mind-generated, imaginary picture of reality you that you forsee.

Try to recollect a time when you trembled in fear about something imaginary and bad that was going to happen with you. Before anything wrong has happened, your thinking generates the feelings and emotions of fear in your head.

Therefore, the root cause is your thinking in a particular pattern. But now you would argue that you on your own didn't think in that particular way, rather, the thoughts crept into your head from anywhere and everywhere. And with these bombarding thoughts, you then find yourself trapped as a victim of fear.

By now, you also have realized that your thoughts are generated primarily from your surrounding environment. If your parents, siblings, spouse, or friends have fearful thoughts, then you would soon find yourself to be thinking that way unless you make some effort on your own to make your thoughts better.

One of the most significant tools to see your thinking and to clear your head is through meditation. You would notice that meditation is no longer considered merely as a means toward spiritual progress. Rather, it is used by top-notch high achievers on a regular basis to sharpen their thinking ability, improve focus, and fine-tune decision-making skills.

So don't skip this chapter thinking that it is something about spiritual stuff that will take you far away from the practical world. No, nothing like that. I am mindful that you have to pay your bills, honor your mortgage, educate your children well, and all this requires you to live in this material world. In fact, due to this very reason, I am recommending this practice of meditation.

So you are with me still? I hope you are. So let's get into this now.

First of all, what do you understand about meditation?

I consider meditation as simply staying in silence and observing your body's movements, breath, and also trying to look at your thoughts going on in your head. I am not suggesting that you should sit in some 'yoga asana' posture to get into meditation. If you are simply walking in the woods, fully aware about your body, able to smell the nature, feel the touch of the cool breeze on your face, observe what's going on in your head, you are already meditating.

But, if you want to get much better benefits, it is always better to still your body. Because, as Ram Dass rightly says *"**The quieter you become, the more you hear.**"* Here we are talking about how to overcome your thoughts of fear of failure, which is a matter of serious concern, as it is plaguing you to take any further action. Therefore it is better if you could spare a minimum dedicated amount of time on a regular basis to get the benefits. Later, I will explain some tools and techniques to get into a meditative state. But before that, let's understand how meditation will really help you to clear your head.

Let me put it very simply. Just think about a glass of water with some sand being put into it. You will see that the water is dirty now. But if you keep the glass still for a minute or so, you will see that all the dust starts settling in the base of the glass, and you can see through the glass very clearly. Similarly, when you are in the state of meditation, your disturbing thoughts running in your head start settling down, which help you to become more resourceful.

There is some neuroscience-based data to support that. There are four different types of brainwaves which operate our thinking system: beta, alpha, theta, and delta (there's gamma as well, but for this conversation, let's talk about the four).

Beta is the state our mind is in on a normal working day and is required to be that way. In the beta state, our mind is active, alert, and concentrating. It is required to function normally. 90% of the time we are awake, our mind is in beta state. As much as the beta is critical, it is the alpha state of mind which is the best state to innovate and to be creative. Probably, that's why Isaac Newton was able to understand the law of gravity by merely sitting silently under an apple tree. It is this alpha state of mind that is responsible for the so-called "Aha" moments for most people.

While beta brainwaves help you to stay in fire-fighting mode and in the mindset of resolving problems, it is the alpha brainwaves that contribute to out-of-box thinking, creativity, and innovation.

Like this morning, when I was meditating (I do it for six minutes after having my bath and just before breakfast), I was able to see the wonderful cover design of this book in front of me. Alpha state puts you in a more creative and resourceful state of mind. See the impact of alpha waves (in yellow), which make your brain more resourceful.

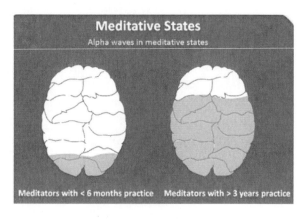

Meditation also stimulates both the major long-term and short-term memory-associated brain regions. The hippocampus and frontal lobe of the brain both light up during meditation. By flexing your memory muscle in meditation, your information storage mechanisms multiply, ensuring that your brain retains the ability to store new memories now and as you age.

How does this all help in conquering the fear of failure?

I would say it helps in multiple ways. First, it brings you in the state of relaxation and opens up a new world of possibilities and resourcefulness for you. Secondly, if you have enhanced memory through meditation, it will help you see the right piece of information in your mind whenever needed.

Once you start getting cues from the universe, supported by the enhanced memory of whatever positive information you are consuming, you get into a more productive state of mind. With enhanced memory and intuitive signals, you are better equipped to start taking action immediately. On the other hand, lack of meditation keeps you in a distracted state and incapable of coming out with a cohesive and thoughtful approach about actions to be taken—and the natural outcome is getting into a fearful state, which plagues your decision and any further action.

In a nutshell, meditation will help you by presenting an alternative and positive viewpoint of any situation.

******

6. Visualize Your Castle To Build it Faster

"Whatever we plant in our subconscious mind and nourish with repetition and emotion will one day become a reality." ~ Earl Nightingale

Everything real on this earth that is created by a human being is first visualized in the human mind. I bet there is no exception to this. Whether it is a small needle or space rockets, everything was first visualized in the human mind before it was materialized.

Whenever you have failed to achieve anything significant in your life, there had been multiple factors responsible for it. A lot many times, there would have been circumstances responsible for it, but also there must have been times when your thinking or visualization in a negative manner would have made it negative for you, before you even started.

I remember a specific personal example of me visualizing myself in a negative way and bore the brunt of that. Here is the instance:

I was in the midst of taking my examination to obtain certain professional qualifications. It was a continual four-days examination—one each day for three hours. The first day went very well. I was super excited, which seems like a genuine reaction if you are confident of your efforts. But my motivation was at the super high levels—rather more than required. In the surge of high motivation, my younger 22-year-old self thought that the second day should be even better than that. So I continued preparing for the exam very late into the night. The next morning, I had to wake up early to reach the examination center.

But this additional effort proved to be more harmful than helpful. Now I realize why people say that you should relax during exams. During those three hours of examination, I was not able to exactly recollect the answers that I was confident in—thanks to sleep deprivation from the night before. I didn't remember what I wrote, but I kept on writing.

Finally, I was done with my second day of exams and in a sad mood thinking that I had failed this time. My mental situation got so negative that I was literally thinking of not going for the remaining two days of the exam. One of my friends told me in a carefree way to forget about what happened and invited me to go out and celebrate the New Year. It was December 31 that day. I tried to control my feelings since my exams continued the next morning. But I ended up wandering the road on my bike with my friend until 2 a.m.

Next morning, I woke up haphazardly at 8 a.m., and then my conscious told me to run for the examination, and I did. But since I had visualized my failure even before attempting, I didn't even have a glance at the preparation material. Finally, I finished the third and last day of the exam.

Two months later, the result was out, and I was holding my head in hands and repenting. I noted that the second day, which I was thinking had gone badly was in fact not that bad. I scored the passing marks. But in the third day, I did not pass it.

I learned from this that even if you think something has turned out badly, you should not imagine that the future would be bad. Because if you think that the future is going to be bad, you will see that the results turn out to be negative. Why? Because you could not focus on your goal and you invited failure.

Above was the example of negative visualization. Now we will talk about positive visualization.

Creative Visualization

I have experimented and tested creative visualization. Though I haven't exactly reached there yet, I have started seeing the glimpse of possibilities for me. I will tell you what I have been visualizing and how far I have gotten. It is not a super success story, but just to build upon the point that wherever you and I are today in our lives is based on what we had been able to think and visualize in our past.

I belong to a third tier city in India. I didn't have the most wonderful schooling. I was good at my studies, and while studying, I generally visualized that I would be working with a top multinational company, wearing a suit and a tie. I didn't know how exactly I would reach there, but studying hard seemed to be the closest approach and the right first step for me. It took me a decade in my career to work for a top multinational corporation with decent car and house. I was sort of living what I had visualized since my early childhood.

But there is a problem with dreams, which is that one keeps on changing his dreams once the former dreams are achieved. Now, due to my inquisitiveness, I found myself exploring the people in the online entrepreneurial world, who were spreading their unique message to uplift humanity at large at the global level and also earning a good living from this. So now my dream had become a different one. I took the courageous step and decided to apply myself full time to the entrepreneurial world after leaving my corporate career. Now, I am happy to see some good results, as recently I was ranked among the top 100 authors at Amazon in the business category with multiple bestselling books. Let me tell you what I was doing during these last few years to reach this stage (I know, it is just beginning and lot more has yet to come).

I was visualizing myself living that dream consistently. That is, I visualized myself creating content that spreads around the world and getting paid for that as well. It is important to remember that there is the only difference of 'time' and 'space,' between the inner world and the outside manifestation. Moreover, the 'time' and 'space' also can be significantly reduced depending upon the level of your intensity of your emotions and consequent actions.

I also took an online course on guided creative visualization meditation from Lisa Nicholas to get deeper into my mind and to see the vivid images of what I wanted to achieve (those images continue to emerge in my head as motivators toward my dream). The only condition for this creative visualization exercise is that if you want to quicken the results, don't give your brain mixed signals. I mean to say, don't switch between having faith and doubting yourself. It won't do you any good. If you are into it, be there and experiment fully. If you imagine something and have a strong desire, you will get it very soon for sure.

So above were my examples of how visualization has affected me adversely as well benefitted me positively in the past few years.

In the movie *Secret*, if you have seen it, you would have seen many examples of the law of attraction working in the achievement of goals. Visualization is a necessary ingredient in the law of attraction. John Assaraf, a self-made multi-millionaire and best-selling author tells about his personal story of visualization's effect. He used to imagine a specific type of big luxurious house in his visualization process with vivid images of bedrooms, living rooms, etc. Though, at that time, it was seemingly out of his financial reach. But he continued the visualization and only after a few years, he found himself living in the same luxurious house of his dreams. That's the power of visualization in attaining your goals. Though it doesn't remove the hurdles coming your way, it insulates you from getting distracted, as your subconscious mind is already focused on suggesting you the resources to make the dream reality. You will find this blog from John Assaraf on the power of visualization at http://johnassaraf.com/law-of-attraction/understand-your-brain-to-use-visualization.

So let's understand what visualization is and how to do it

Visualization is a relaxation technique in which you imagine pleasant scenarios or scenes. There are two basic ways you can use visualization to overcome fear. One, you can visualize yourself overcoming the fear, which will eventually translate to real life success. You can also visualize a calming scenario in moments of intense fear.

Don't think that this is like daydreaming. I would say, you already had been daydreaming but dreaming negatively about something going wrong. Why do you think that thinking negatively is the norm and a practical approach like visualizing positive things is like daydream?

You are not entirely at fault. As a part of society, which often tells you, "*Hey, don't fly. Come on the ground. You are not like that. You won't be able to achieve that. It is too difficult. Your circumstances are not in our favor etc. etc."* So you get sold on these statements.

Remember, visualization is very powerful. The brain's response to imagined scenarios is often on par with its response to real life success and failure[xii]. If you want to overcome fear, it can be helpful to make a point of habitually visualizing yourself succeeding. But don't overdo it. Try to keep your scenario realistic. Imagine yourself overcoming your fear in a manner that could happen. Imagine things going reasonably well. Picture yourself staying calm and collected while in front of the adverse situation. Imagine your heart rate remaining relatively stable and remaining calm.

So, when you have to deal with something that frightens you, try to visualize regularly. Close your eyes and imagine success. Take ten to fifteen minutes before bed each night to visualize yourself overcoming your fear. You may find yourself becoming calmer in real life if you regularly face your fears in your mind. For example, you may speak more calmly at regular work meetings.

---

xii

https://www.psychologytoday.com/blog/flourish/200912/seeing-is-believing-the-power-visualization

If you continuously play that mental movie of overcoming the fear of failure, you will shortly be getting a glimpse of wisdom from the universe. Now once you start getting that, your role is to put some action into it, and soon you will see your fear leaving forever.

So the mantra is:

Visualize >> invite the universal cues >> trust and take action >> overcome the fear

Action cures the fear, we all know. But visualization is something that will put you into action.

"The key to effective visualization is to create the most detailed, clear and vivid picture to focus on as possible. The more vivid the visualization, the more likely and more quickly, you are to begin attracting the things that help you achieve what you want to get done." ~ Georges St. Pierre

****

7. Reverse Brainwash Yourself

"Everyone is a genius. But if you judge a fish by its ability to climb a tree, it will live its whole life believing that it is stupid." Albert Einstein

Please don't get offended when I say that a major part of the society is already brainwashed to some extent. I don't see myself as an exception to that. Our society brainwashes us to live a life of mediocrity. In the name of religion, staying poor is shown as a virtue. Earning more money is shown as greed.

Have you ever dared to challenge these thoughts? Have you ever questioned the society for creating this belief system? Have you ever thought why it is that to live your life you have to listen more to the voices of the people around you? Did you ever think that perhaps louder voices were coming from within you that you have neglected?

Who made you think that the voices coming from around you is the right voice and the inner noise is wrong? Do you think that if so many people keep on saying one thing, that thing becomes right?

If you think that there is something inside you that you have been suppressing from ages , you need to ask these tough questions. You don't need to always suppress your inner voice from the loud voices from the people around you.

I remember watching a movie scene a few years ago. The scene was something like this. There was a hot argument going on between father and son. It was a family scene, and the argument was due to the disagreement of the marriage of the protagonist with a poor girl, whom he loved. In the rage of anger, Father throws an empty glass on the floor. The son remained calm and did something, which was a firm and courageous move.

He asked a servant standing there to get a tray of empty glasses kept nearby. He picked up one glass and threw it on the floor. The father was shocked. The son picks up another glass and again throws it on the floor. Same with the third glass. One by one, the son throws all the glasses on the floor and then there was silence.

Now the son says, "Dad, if by breaking the glass on the floor and by shouting, you think your argument becomes stronger, then I have now broken six glasses, so does breaking more glasses makes my argument stronger than yours?"

What did you get out of this? The message I took was that even if the noise outside is louder and so many people are doing a particular thing, that does not always mean that they are right. If you agree with the views of the society, that's fine. But if you disagree personally, then merely agreeing to what others say is just a compromise. It is like suppressing your own individuality. By not living the way you want to live, what are you gaining? Of course, you stay in the comfort zone, but you don't shine.

What is the solution to get rid of the negative beliefs about fear in trying something you wanted? So far, society has been brainwashing you with its mediocre and frightening thoughts. Now I ask you to brainwash yourself to nullify the effect of the negative brainwashing. In fact, I had put my best shot to reverse brainwash myself. I have lived enough years the way society wants all of us to live. I have seen the three necessary phases of change in one's thought process and mindset.

Phase I- You naturally feel that what society says is correct, and you blindly follow that.

Phase II- You start encountering some life realities, and then you internally feel that there is some disconnect in the way you want to lead your life and the way society's belief systems work. (Based on my interactions with people, I know that the majority feels this way at some point of time in life, unless he or she is already listening and acting according to their heart's desires.)

Phase III- Either you jumpstart and take some action to change the things on your own or the circumstances push you against the wall so hard that you take the plunge to take a different route contrary to the norms of society.

After going through all the three phases and getting myself reverse-brainwashed positively for more than a decade, it became a no-brainer for me to develop my own faith and listen to my own inner voice. In fact, my own positive brainwashing has helped me to write multiple books at a faster pace. The majority of people stop at Phase II, despite realizing the harsh realities, because going to Phase III takes courage.

If you are being pushed against the wall too much, then brainwashing is something will help you to put you on track faster.

We will call this *reverse brainwashing,* because brainwashing is generally construed as a negative thing, so it feels better to call this as reverse brainwashing.

I hope you are convinced and ready to get reverse brainwashed now. So let's understand how best and how soon you can get brainwashed. There are free resources, inexpensive books, as well as paid online courses to effectively help you change your mindset. Despite being free and inexpensive, don't undermine the value of the nuggets of wisdom shared there.

The resources include freely available podcasts, YouTube videos, and books that will help you develop your mindset faster. I know the pain of slow progress and how it kills daily, so I would recommend fast tracking your progress.

It is like giving your body a strong dose of a vitamin that you lack. I had some medical tests done in the past. The reports showed that there is a deficiency of vitamin D in the body. It was not too much lower, but the doctor advised two options. Option one was to take some tablets of vitamin D for a continuous three to six months. Option two was to take 600,000 units of vitamin D through injection at one go.

So, you have to choose, if there is something deficient, which route you will choose? You can start immediately immersing yourself in positive literature, or you may take a slower approach to reading five pages of a book per day. I leave it up to you. You have to decide your requirement of reverse brainwashing and take action accordingly.

There are free podcasts to start with. I recommend the following to get some insights into how your inner psychology works and how these will help you to overcome your fear of failure.

a. Fear Not
b. The Life Coach School
c. Optimize with Brian Johnson
d. Entrepreneur on Fire (if you want inspiration to start your business)

YouTube Videos:

You should subscribe to the following YouTube channels to continually get your dose of material to change your neuropathways:

a. Mastery Session by Robin Sharma
b. Tom Bilyeu
c. Brendon Burchard

The best tool is Google, where you can seek our necessary guidance on any question you have. But the central idea is that you need to feed your brain with something else to overpower your negative conditioning of your mind. Once the upgraded belief systems get installed in your mind, you will find yourself more solution-oriented rather than feeling stress and anxiety about the outcome.

8. Worst-Case & Best-Case Assessment & Get Going Faster

"For every failure, there's an alternative course of action. You just have to find it. When you come to a roadblock, take a detour." Mary Kay Ash

What does your fear of failure do?

We already discussed that it scares the hell out of you and cripples you to take the next step. You put a magnifying glass on your fear and you see the worst-case scenario, like a tsunami heading towards you with a devastating pace.

Imagine you have a crucial meeting with key customers of your company, or you have to give a presentation to a group of investors of your company. The stakes are really high in this case, and any lapse in your preparation may cost dearly to your company. You are scared because you don't want to fail and feel bad. Your brain is so well-trained that it keeps you at your basic survival level. It doesn't want to put you in any risky situation. It suggests that if you take some active role in the discussions, you might say something wrong, which will adversely impact you. Therefore, you choose not to participate in the discussion effectively and maintain a low profile to remain safe.

If the above corporate-like environment doesn't fit your circumstances, you may substitute it with another example. It could be like preparing for your big examination, starting out a new venture in your life, or putting a big-ticket investment in some area. It could be anything that scares you. The fear of failure comes in such a way that your palms are wet and your forehead sweats, just like if your life was in danger.

But now you are wiser. You already know that this fear is indeed a beacon towards your bigger goals. Here is a simple way to avoid getting distracted by the fear and start moving.

Take a pen and paper, or your keyboard. Think about two different extreme scenarios, which may turn out as an outcome of your situation.

    a.   The Worst-Case Scenario
    b.   The Best-Case Scenario

Look at the worst-case scenario and assess the maximum amount of damage that can happen to you if you take action. Now, if you think that the worst-case scenario is something that is not going to be a blunder, then go for it. As a reasonable person, you can understand the difference between a mistake and a blunder. Something can be stated as a mistake or a blunder depending on the nature of the negative outcome generated from it.

In other words, a mistake is something that can be easily reversed and at a lower cost. So you can do it over again. But a blunder is something that is catastrophic. It is like jumping off the cliff knowing that you will die, and if you survived, you will have difficulty recovering.

So whenever you come across the fear of failure, you have to ascertain the worst-case scenario. Depending upon what stage of life you are at, your definition of worst-case scenarios will differ. If you are just out of college, you can take a much bigger risk and venture out. You know that even after the worst-case scenario occurs, you will still get a job, as you have a qualifications. But if you are in the middle of your career and have many responsibilities on your hands, you probably need to be extra cautious and careful in measuring your worst-case scenario.

I was attending a conference a few years ago and heard an interview of Rohit Bansal, co-founder of SnapDeal, an Indian E-commerce company. He told us that when he and his co-founder, Kunal Bahl, decided to start the company, both were working in a corporate world with a decent salary. While deciding to start their first venture in 2008, they did a worst-case scenario analysis. Both decided that they had the necessary professional qualifications and experience of the corporate world and had some savings. They thought that if they start some venture and it doesn't turn out to be a success, what was the worst-case scenario? They were able to conclude that at the max, they would lose out all their savings, but they would be able to go back to their jobs and get settled again.

But, they also thought about the best-case scenario as well. The best-case scenario was to take a ride on the internet and E-commerce boom happening in India. It was an innovative step in the country, and they realized that they would be amongst the front-runners in this game. They were mindful that if they can set up an E-commerce platform, there was an opportunity to get outside funding and business could go through the roof. And that's what has happened. SnapDeal turned out to be a mega success and both the promoters have gained rich experiences and huge financial rewards out of their decision.

Above was an example of taking action after considering both the worst and best scenarios. These two people realized that whatever they would do, it was reversible with some cost of losing their savings and then again returning to their old life. Assuming they had remained fearful and had not taken that initial plunge, they would have been living a routine corporate employee job, which would last at least sixty years.

Gary Vaynerchuk, an American entrepreneur and bestselling author, once surveyed a large number of people older than sixty years of age. They were asked about one thing they regretted in their life. The answer was almost in all cases a very emotional and painful picture of what they felt. Most people said that their biggest regret was not at least trying what was lying in their heart. It was a realization that life is not about always playing it safe and comfortable. It is more about evolving as a human being, which happens if you go out of your comfort zone.

Please try to understand that fear gets inflated if you are clouded in your thinking. It portrays life-threatening situations even before you try it. The moment you start to think more precisely about the best-case and worst-case scenarios, you start to see the initial action point in a very short time.

This strategy has always worked for me. I have also left my corporate job at the age of forty-two with a full responsibility of my family with two kids. But I know for myself the best-case scenario would be having the entire world as my audience to listen to my message. I also know the worst-case scenario and know that I may get back to what I was doing earlier (which is only the last resort, if nothing works out). Although this might seem like a blunder from the outside world, I would consider it only as a reversible mistake at the max with a cost associated with it.

So, my friend, try to differentiate between a mistake and a blunder. Don't let yourself feel regret due to your fear of failure. You just need to calculate the worst-case scenario and cost, while focussing your attention on the blue ocean of possibilities that you may come across. It will make it easier for you to take steps to overcome the fear of failure.

Therefore, make your plans and take actions because:

"Action is the fundamental key to all success." ~ Pablo Picasso

****

9. Master Your Intuition to Take Inspired Action

"Intuition is the discriminative faculty that enables you to decide which of the two lines of reasoning is right. Perfect intuition makes you master of all."
~Paramahansa Yogananda

As I stated somewhere else in this book already, all our body functions happen on its own without any intervention from our side. We didn't make our body, God created it, and therefore God is running this machinery on its own. You have no control over your breathing or your cardiac function; you don't have any role in the digestion of your food and circulation of blood in your body. Your brain works on its own to perform all bodily functions.

It is obvious, so why I am stating all this? There is a reason. We trust in the supreme power of all our body function and don't ever interfere with it. But there is one more unique resource from the universe, which we mostly fail to utilize and take benefit from. We ignore the unique cues from the universe, which are mostly for our good if we are able to hear them properly.

Yes, you guessed it right. I am talking about what you call a "gut" feeling or a "hunch" or in a refined way, *intuition*. We have been given a mind and a consciousness to utilize in the best way for our ultimate good. But your mind is a double-edged sword. You can use it to safeguard yourself from your enemies and defeat your enemies or you can harm yourself with this sword.

Okay, let me put it this way. I am talking about a human mind being like a sword. Most of the population pollutes the mind it with negative emotions, fear being one of the prime ones. On the other hand, intuition is a direct message from the universe to help us out in guiding our life like a GPS. Unfortunately, to us human beings, life decisions don't appear to be so simple like breathing, digesting, pumping of blood in the body etc., so whenever we are in a difficult situation, we cloud our heads with the thoughts of fear, stress, and anxiety, which make us incapable to hear our intuition.

"Have the courage to follow your heart and intuition. They somehow already know what you truly want to become."
~ Steve Jobs

Let me tell you, fear and intuition are the gifts given to us that allow us to navigate life. Like our internal GPS, they help us steer through the often murky journey of endless decisions we make each day. But they do it in different ways. Intuition can tell us "yes" or "no," but fear only ever says "no."

Intuition exists solely in the present moment, about the present moment. It is a quick flash from our subconscious mind which, if unrecognized or drowned out by logic or fear, can fade away as quickly as it came. It is sometimes strong, but more often gentle. It usually presents itself as a physical sensation (a "gut" feeling), vision or image, before words or concrete facts comes into focus. It feels sure—until you doubt it (and that may be within a matter of seconds).

How Do You Distinguish Between Intuition and Fear and Listen to Your Gut Feeling?

It's easy to confuse fear for intuition because it can also come on quickly, and be experienced physically. But there are some major differences.

How do you know it is intuition?

- It feels like a 'knowing' more than a logical or highly emotional response.

- The message is felt or heard instantly; the message is fluid and non-repetitive.
- The message feels definitive, almost like the answer is black or white and doesn't require analyzing.
- The message feels simple and comfortable; it may also feel "right."
- The message feels loving and supportive, almost expansive.
- The message is centered around the present moment.
- You feel a wave of joy.

How does fear look different?

- Fear isn't subtle. It's usually relentless, painful, cruel, repetitive, and full of details.
- Fear proves its point by referencing the past and projects a lot of its focus into the future.
- Fear feels bad, uncomfortable, and since it activates the brain's amygdala, it stimulates the fight, flight, or freeze response.
- The message seems to have many variables and "what ifs," which can lead to confusion or feeling stuck.
- The message feels very harsh or restrictive.

- The message is usually centered around the future or scenarios that have not yet happened.

Fear is important; it's designed to keep us safe. But for most of us, our fear is in overdrive—overriding our intuition and exaggerating the threat of danger. That's okay, as long as you recognize it when that's happening. The real problem is when we mistake our fear for intuition and then let it run the show. When fear leads, the journey continues, but the ride is bumpier and scarier.

How do you encourage that gentle wisdom of intuition to push past the dreading fear of failure?

- Keep a clear mind; a clear mind is more receptive to intuitive messages whereas a cluttered and distracted mind is more susceptible to fear-based messages.

- Identify whether it is fear or intuition using your feelings and not logic.

- If you have identified fear, work on acknowledging and calming your thoughts using rationality or meditative practices, it is better *to wait for the emotions to settle before taking action.*

- If you have identified intuition, *take appropriate actions to follow through on your feelings*, if still unsure, trust that the message will reveal itself in time.

There are no definitive boundaries between fear and intuition. The only thing you can do is learn to trust and love yourself, because the more you can do that, the more you develop your capacity to listen to messages from the universe.

I had taken an online course of Sonia Choquette, who is an expert in teaching how to develop intuition. You can learn more about Sonia Choquette and her teaching material at http://www.positiveintuition.com/lp.

As you notice that intuition appears as a spark of light and vanishes quickly too is the moment you start doubting the inspiration arisen by your intuition. So the best advice is to feel the intuition and immediately take some action on that.

"Improvisation is intuition in action, a way to discover the muse and learn to respond to her call." ~Stephen Nachmanovitch

****

10. Make Your Fears Tangible & Thrash Them Out

"Keeping a journal of what's going on in your life is a good way to help you distill what's important and what's not." ~ Martina Navratilova

I am a big fan of journaling, thanks to Robin Sharma's miraculous book *The Monk Who Sold His Ferrari*, which wonderfully explains the importance of journaling in improving our lives.

I personally follow this journaling tool on a daily basis with a standard set of questions. If you are new to journaling, let me give you a brief explanation and perspective on it. I personally see the journal as my second mind outside of my mind. Second mind because whatever thoughts wander in your head, you get them out on paper or your laptop. So journaling helps to declutter your mind make room for the fresh air and fresh perspective.

The second point I want to make is you can fight an enemy only if it is visible and tangible in front of you. Through journaling, you literally give your negative thoughts, fear included, a physical shape. Now you can clearly see your thought and take some action based on it.

Lastly, journaling helps you to identify the problem more conclusively. You would have already realized that thoughts, if not written, continue to hound around in your mind. The different neurons in your brain keep on forming different neuro-connections, and one thought leads to another. By the time you realize, you are already in the myriad of confusing thoughts aggravating your fear and anxiety. So journaling helps you to see all those thoughts in front of you.

In fact, if you are serious about overcoming the fear of failure, you should quickly start your journal. It should precisely be a *"Fear Journal."* It is another form of a journal, but with a specific focus on understanding your fear deeply to help you get the cues to overcome those fears.

How does writing your fear journal help you?

a. It helps to get the fear out. Just remember that your fears have much more power over you when they are inside your head. Writing them down undermines this power right away, and it might feel like a weight being taken off.

b. You can see it from a distance. Writing puts the fear outside your mind. Now you can separate yourself from the chaos of it, and see it for what it is. You know how other people's fear don't seem so bad to you? One person is afraid of falling from height, while another is terribly frightened of talking to strangers. The two almost wish they had the other's fear because "that would be easier than what I have." The distance gives you a new perspective. You can do that to your own fears. Sometimes from this distance, you can see how ridiculous your fear appears. Other times, with this new perspective, you can have some space to make a plan of action.

What to write in your Fear Journal:

There is no one way to make a fear journal, but here are some ideas:

1. Write in a stream of conscious to get it all out. Whatever comes to you, write it down.
2. Write a list of your fears and/or the tricks and tactics to conquer them.
3. Write down where they came from and/or what holds them there (i.e., what evidence you have that they are "true").
4. Write down how you know they are not true.

5. Write down what is precious behind the fear.
6. Make a plan to express that preciousness in other ways (e.g., if you fear losing your mom, spend more time with her).
7. Write a goodbye letter to the fear. You can be as elaborate in that letter as you want and request the fear to go away from your life. This formal action putting it to paper will strengthen your intention of getting rid of fear. It will send positive signals to your mind to change its way. I found a well-intentioned goodbye letter sample, which you may like to read.
8. Take an inventory of your skills and knowledge, which you can use to overcome any specific fear.

Natalie Goldberg, speaker and author explains what you should write:

"Write what disturbs you. What you fear, what you have not been willing to speak about. Be willing to be split open."

****

11. You Can Turn Fear Into Exhilaration with This

"Your calm mind is the ultimate weapon against your challenges, so relax." ~ Bryant McGill

How would you react if you knew that you can convert your fears into excitement by one simple technique? Not only that—this excitement can lead to exhilaration once you go one level further.

Don't get shocked by the mere simplicity of this tactic (I was amazed to hear this when I first heard it)! Also, don't underestimate the power of this method merely because it is simple.

While listening to Gay Hendricks's wonderful book, *The Big Leap—Conquer Your Hidden Fear and Take Your Life to the Next Level*, I was exposed to this simple technique.

Hendricks explains that fear is nothing but lack of breath in your brain. So what is the technique: **Breathe Into Your Fear**

Hendricks goes on to explain in his book (here is the relevant extract from the book):

"There's only one way to get through the fog of fear, and that's to transform it into the clarity of exhilaration. One of the greatest pieces of wisdom I've ever heard comes from Fritz Perls, MD, the psychiatrist and founder of Gestalt therapy. He said, 'Fear is excitement without the breath.' Here's what this intriguing statement means: the very same mechanisms that produce excitement also produce fear, and any fear can be transformed into excitement by breathing fully with it. On the other hand, excitement turns into fear quickly if you hold your breath. When scared, most of us have a tendency to try to get rid of the feeling. We think we can get rid of it by denying or ignoring it, and we use holding our breath as a physical tool of denial.

It never works, though, because as Dr. Perls has pointed out, the less breath you feed your fear, the bigger your fear gets. The best advice I can give you is to take big, easy breaths when you feel fear. Feel the fear instead of pretending it's not there. Celebrate it with a big breath, just the way you'd celebrate your birthday by taking a big breath and blowing out all the candles on your cake. Do that, and your fear turns into excitement. Do it more, and your excitement turns into exhilaration."

Then I went to do some more research to find some resources from *Fritz Perls, MD about Gestalt therapy*[xiii]. And I noted one clarification about what breathe means. He explains as follows:

".......know that breathing means exhaling. There is a fetish in our time about breathing, the big chest, the he-man fetish that thinks breathing is inhaling. But breathing means throwing out the bad air. You would not go to a basin and wash your hands with the water, dirty water, half full in the basin. And you don't pour clean water on top of it. Now the same with breathing. First get rid of the bad air, the carbon dioxide, and then bring in the fresh air. If you can do this, the acute state of anxiety, or asthma, will very quickly disappear. As a matter of fact, in asthma, you often see children forcefully exhaling, 'Wwhueeeue . . .' 'whueeeue . . .' Thus nature takes over."

I practiced this breathing technique, and it made me think, *Yes, this thing works.* The more I focused on the breath—not merely focused rather tried to take deeper breathes into the depth of my stomach and exhaling fully; it felt quite relieving. It was surprising

xiii

http://gestalttheory.com/persons/fritzperls/public ations/finding-self-through-gestalt-therapy/

that merely getting the deeper breath and full exhaling induces relaxation in the brain. So the next question was how come breathing into the stomach brings results like peace and relaxation into the brain? How could such long breathing push away the negative emotions of fear or anxiety and bring in joy?

So I dug deeper and further and found a very interesting scientific fact related to the stomach as well. Let me state that here as well.

If you don't know already, the human body has a second brain in the stomach in our gut or alimentary canal, which contains some 100 million neurons, more than in either the spinal cord or the peripheral nervous system. Also, 95% of the primary brain chemical, serotonin, also known as the "happy chemical," is found in the bowel areas of human body. A big part of our emotions is probably influenced by the nerves in our gut. Scientists say that butterflies in the stomach— signaling in the gut as part of our physiological stress response, is but one example.[xiv]

Also, traditional Chinese medicine recognizes the significance of stomach areas as the center of energy of human beings. They say that a

xiv

https://www.scientificamerican.com/article/gut-second-brain/

person should find their center to restore their health and energy. What they mean by this is bringing your awareness to the stomach region, which is a major energy center.[xv]

I have tried this breathing exercise a number of times. It is in fact a type of meditation itself, as meditation is also concentrating on some specific activity of your body.

Next time you feel fearful to take action, use this breathing technique to calm down your mind and soon you will find yourself in a different state of excitement. In that state of mind, you will start improving the receptacle of your mind to be more resourceful, and your thoughts will lead you to the right set of people and opportunities to work with, rather than be infected with the inaction and indecision bug.

"The quality of our breath expresses our inner feelings." ~ TKV Desikachar

******

[xv] https://www.mindbodygreen.com/0-4717/Overcome-Fear-with-a-Simple-Breathing-Exercise.html

Final Words

"There is only one thing that makes a dream impossible to achieve: the fear of failure." ~ Paulo Coelho

So finally, this book has come to a close. Before we part ways, however, I want to tell you how much I appreciate you reading this book.

You and I know there is a vast majority of people around who simply express their concerns or problems, but rarely do anything to find a solution and move ahead. You belong to a small minority of people who really care about their dreams. Finishing this book means that you're committed to changing yourself.

If you opened this book unsure about how to deal with the fear of failure and take action, I hope that now you understand that it's you who defines what failure is and you can very well make every failure a stepping stone to your success.

Just like you can use a knife for two entirely different purposes—to take somebody's life or to prepare them a healthy meal—you can either treat failure as a reason to give up and never try again or as a teacher that helps you correct your course and keep moving.

But the choice always remains in your hands— you can continue to wear your old lenses and see the failure as a frightening monster or stand up, clean up your glasses, remove the dust of negative beliefs, and take charge of your life. The latter is my wish for you.

I am wishing for your success in all your dreams.

Cheers,

Som Bathla

Thank You!

Before you go, I would like to say thank you for purchasing and reading my book.

You could have picked amongst dozens of other books on this subject, but you took a chance and checked out this one.

So, big thanks for downloading this book and reading all the way to the end.

Now I'd like to ask for a small favor. **Could you please spend a minute or two and leave a review for this book on Amazon?**

This feedback will help me continue to write the kind of Kindle books that help you get results.

Made in United States
North Haven, CT
18 October 2021

10410585R00106